Norman Dello Joio

Twayne's Music Series

Norman Dello Joio

Thomas A. Bumgardner

Twayne Publishers
A Division of G. K. Hall & Co. • Boston

Norman Dello Joio

Thomas A. Bumgardner

Copyright © 1986
By G. K. Hall & Co.
All Rights Reserved
Published by Twayne Publishers
A Division of G. K. Hall & Co.
70 Lincoln Street
Boston, Massachusetts 02111

First Printing

Photograph of Norman Dello Joio
courtesy of Boston University Photo Service

Copyediting supervised by Lewis DeSimone
Book design by Barbara Anderson
Book production by Elizabeth Todesco

Typeset in 10 pt. Century Oldstyle by
Compset, Inc. of Beverly Massachusetts

Printed on permanent/durable acid-free paper
and bound in the United States of America

Library of Congress Cataloging in Publication Data

Bumgardner, Thomas A. (Thomas Arthur), 1942–
Norman Dello Joio.

(Twayne's music series)
Bibliography: p. 159
"Catalog of musical works": p. 164
Discography: p. 171
Includes index.
1. Dello Joio, Norman, 1913–   . 2. Composers—United States—
Biography. 3. Dello Joio, Norman, 1913–   —Criticism and
interpretation.   I. Title. II. Series.
ML410.D353B8   1986   780'.92'4 [B]   85-27236
ISBN 0-8057-9465-4

In memory of my Parents

Contents

About the Author

Thomas Arthur Bumgardner was born in Houston, Texas, on 30 September 1942, the son of Genevieve Bumgardner and Ned Bumgardner. After graduation from Reagan High School, Houston, Texas, in 1960, he entered North Texas State University at Denton, Texas. He received the degree of Bachelor of Arts with a major in music in January 1964. In September 1964 he entered the Graduate School of the University of Minnesota–Minneapolis. He was awarded the degree of Master of Fine Arts in August 1966. In September 1966 he joined the music faculty at the University of Wisconsin-Superior where he is currently professor of music and coordinator of the music program. During the summer of 1968, he enrolled in the Graduate School of the University of Texas at Austin, to begin his doctoral studies. In 1969–70 he took a leave-of-absence from the University of Wisconsin–Superior in order to devote full time to graduate studies. He completed his graduate work in August 1973 and was awarded the Doctor of Musical Arts degree. The subject of his doctoral treatise was *The Solo Vocal Works of Norman Dello Joio*.

Dr. Bumgardner is a baritone who has appeared often in recital, opera, and oratorio performances in the upper Midwest. He is married to Rena Jewell of Athens, Texas. They reside in Superior, Wisconsin, with their three daughters, Melody, Susan, and Judi.

Preface

As we enter the twilight years of the twentieth century, we are in a position to reflect on those persons and events that have had a significant impact on the shaping of contemporary American musical culture. Yet if the average person were asked to give a list of American composers of serious music, he or she might be able to name two or three, such as Leonard Bernstein and Aaron Copland. Even though for the last half century the music of American composers has ranked with the best the world has to offer, the fact is that we in America still know more about the music of Western Europe (roughly that of Bach through Stravinsky) than we know about our own. The intent of Twayne's Music Series is to rectify that situation by taking a close look at specific individuals who have had a substantial impact on the music of the twentieth century. Emphasis will be on American contributions in classical music, jazz, popular music, and opera.

The subject of this volume is Norman Dello Joio—one of America's leading composers for the past four decades. Any attempt to relate the contributions of American composers to the music of this century would be remiss if it did not take into account the work of this Pulitzer Prize-winning composer. Since the late 1940s, Dello Joio has been consistently listed as one of this country's most significant composers. In 1956 a panel from *Music Club Magazine* listed him among the six leading composers of American music. The others were Samuel Barber, Aaron Copland, Peter Mennin, Walter Piston, and William Schuman. In 1963 Dello Joio was featured by the *National Observer* in an article entitled "The Artists Who Create the Nation's Best Serious Music." In addition to the names just mentioned, the article listed Gian-Carlo Menotti, Douglas Moore, and Howard Hanson. In 1966 the Music Educators National Conference (MENC) reported that Dello Joio's compositions for band were performed more often than those of any other composer.

In addition to the many prizes that Dello Joio has won for his compositions, he has been awarded an honorary Doctor of Music degree from four different colleges and universities, and he has been elected to membership in the American Academy of Arts and Letters. He is a prolific composer who has written in all of the traditional genres of serious music—symphonic, choral, opera, chamber, keyboard, vocal, and ballet—and has also written for the modern media of television and film. In addition to his contributions in the field of musical composition, Dello Joio has had a significant impact on the field of music education through his work as Chairman of the Policy Committee for the Ford Foundation Contemporary Music Project.

This book represents the first comprehensive study of Dello Joio's life and work. The first chapter is a biographical study that covers his family background, his birth and childhood experience, the influences that shaped his career and compositional style, and focuses on his most significant accomplishments. The remaining chapters discuss and analyze his music categorically in chronological order. Additional features include a chronological list of compositions and a discography.

During the course of this writing, I have collected and studied all available published material by and about Norman Dello Joio. In addition, I spent four weeks at his home in East Hampton, New York, where I had the opportunity to spend several hours interviewing the man and visiting socially with him and members of his family. Contained in the attic studio of his home are all of his surviving manuscripts—those primary sources that are essential in a study of this type. Although I did use the manuscripts during the course of my study, references in the book are always to the published score because most readers would not have access to the manuscripts. In addition to the manuscripts, the studio contains a letter file dating back to 1940. Unfortunately, Dello Joio did not make a habit of keeping copies of his own letters, so with few exceptions the file contains only letters to Norman Dello Joio, not from him. The study of that material will have to await its collection in a central location. Another source of extremely valuable information was a collection of scrapbooks found in a closet of the attic studio. For a number of years Dello Joio subscribed to a clipping service that furnished news articles about him which appeared anywhere in the country. Grayce Dello Joio, Norman's wife until their divorce in 1971, collected these clippings along with other memorabilia such as concert programs, and arranged them by year in scrapbooks and boxes. Barbara Dello Joio, Norman's wife since 1974, continued this practice. I am indebted to both Grayce and Barbara for saving me many hours of searching and organizing.

As a volume in Twayne's Music Series, this book is written for the general reader, not the music specialist. Therefore I have attempted to keep detailed technical analysis to a minimum, focusing rather on general trends and aspects of style. However, in order to convey to the reader the true essence of the music instead of just peripheral aspects, I was compelled to use a certain amount of technical jargon. While these terms are explained in the text, the reader may wish to consult additional sources such as the *Harvard Dictionary of Music* for further explanation.

Although the principal intent of this book is to engage the interest of the listening public in a fine contemporary composer, that goal would have little chance of being realized if I did not succeed in engaging the interest of the potential interpreter of Dello Joio's music. For no amount of reading about music can substitute for the actual experience of hearing it. Therefore my writing is aimed at least in part toward the performers and conductors of today's concert music. As a musician whose primary training has been in the area of performance rather than theory or musicology, I believe that I can offer a perspective on Dello Joio's music that perhaps someone with a more academic orientation could not.

Finally, because this book is the first to be written about Norman Dello Joio, I hope that it will stimulate additional inquiry into the life and work of a master composer of our time.

Thomas A. Bumgardner

University of Wisconsin–Superior

Acknowledgments

I wish to express appreciation to Norman Dello Joio for his cooperation and encouragement during the research and writing of this book. Having access to the manuscripts, personal papers, and the man himself proved to be most rewarding. I am indebted to him for reading the manuscript, correcting factual errors, and offering his opinions.

I wish to thank both Norman and Barbara Dello Joio for their kind hospitality during my visits to their home. Heartfelt thanks are due to Ray and Jane Oster, who provided housing, food, and transportation for me during my stay on Long Island. I am grateful to the University of Wisconsin–Superior for a summer research grant in support of this project. Thanks are due to Jan Austin for her assistance in typing portions of the manuscript, to Judy Rynne for preparing the musical examples, and to the editorial staff at G. K. Hall for their assistance in the preparation of the manuscript for publication. For their willingness to grant interviews, I wish to thank Grant Beglarian, Donald George, and William Schuman. Finally, I wish to thank my wife and daughters for their loving support, which sustained me during this endeavor.

Excerpts from the following are used by arrangement with G. Schirmer, Inc.: *Songs of Remembrance,* "The Lion House," *Southern Echoes, Duo Concertato, The Ruby,* and *The Trial at Rouen.*

Excerpts from the following are used by permission of Hal Leonard Publishing Corp.: *Take Our Hand Walt Whitman, Capriccio on the Interval of a Second, Laudation, Antiphonal Fantasy, Concertante* for wind instruments, and *Songs of Abelard.*

Excerpts from the following are used by permission of Carl Fischer, Inc.: *Song of the Open Road,* copyright 1953 by Carl Fischer, Inc., © renewed 1981; *Meditations on Ecclesiastes,* © 1959 by Carl Fischer, Inc.; *Concertante* for clarinet and orchestra, copyright 1955 by Carl Fischer, Inc., © renewed 1983; Sonata no. 3 for piano, copyright 1948 by Carl Fischer, Inc., © renewed 1975; and *Air Power,* copyright 1957 by Carl Fischer, Inc.

Chronology

1913 Norman Dello Joio born in New York City 24 January.

1925 Appointed organist/choirmaster at Star of the Sea Church on City Island.

1930 Graduates from All-Hallows Institute in New York City.

1936 Graduates from Institute of Musical Art in New York City.

1937 Trio for piano, violin, and cello wins Elizabeth Sprague Coolidge Award.

1939 Graduates from Juilliard Graduate School.

1941 Appointed Musical Director of Eugene Loring's *Dance Players*.

1942 Weds Grayce Baumgold, 5 June.

1943 *Magnificat* for orchestra wins Town Hall Composition Award.

1945 Succeeds William Schuman as teacher of composition at Sarah Lawrence College.

1946 *Concert Music* for orchestra premiered in Pittsburgh. *Tre Ricercare* for piano and orchestra premiered in New York. Makes concert tour of Poland.

1948 *Variations, Chaconne, and Finale* premiered in Pittsburgh, 30 January (New York Premiere on 9 December).

1949 Wins New York Music Critics Circle Award for *Variations, Chaconne and Finale*.
Concertante for clarinet and orchestra premiered, 22 May at Chautauqua, New York.
New York Profiles premiered, 21 August at La Jolla, California.
Serenade for orchestra premiered, 20 October in Cleveland.

1951 *Triumph of Saint Joan Symphony* premiered in Louisville.

1953 *A Song of Affirmation* premiered at Cornell College in Iowa.

1955 *The Ruby* premiered at Indiana University.

1956 *The Trial at Rouen* premiered on NBC Television, 8 April.
Air Power premiered on CBS Television, 11 November.

1957 Awarded Pulitzer Prize for *Meditations on Ecclesiastes.*

1958 Featured on CBS Television program, "Profile of a Composer."

1959 Wins New York Music Critics Circle Award for *The Triumph of Saint Joan.*
Appointed Chairman of the Selection Committee for the Young Composers Project.

1961 *Blood Moon* premiered by the San Francisco Opera Company.

1962 *Fantasy and Variations* premiered in Cincinnati.

1963 *Variants on a Medieval Tune* premiered at Duke University.
Appointed Chairman of the Project Policy Committee for the Contemporary Music Project.

1964 Toured Russia, Rumania, and Bulgaria for the U. S. State Department.
The Louvre premiered on NBC Television.

1965 Wins Emmy Award for *The Louvre.*
Appointed to Research Advisory Council by U. S. Office of Education.

1966 U. S. representative at Festival of the Arts in this Century in Hawaii.
Songs of Walt Whitman premiered at Interlochen, Michigan, 20 August.
Antiphonal Fantasy premiered in Tulsa, 12 December.

1967 Wins Lancaster Symphony Composers Award.

1968 *Fantasies on a Theme by Haydn* premiered in Michigan.

1969 *Homage to Haydn* premiered in Little Rock.

1972 Appointed Dean of the School of the Arts at Boston University.

1974 Weds Barbara Bolton.

1976 *Colonial Variants* premiered in Wilmington, Delaware.

1977 Southern Echoes premiered in Savannah, Georgia, 22 January.
Songs of Remembrance premiered at Saratoga Performing Arts Center, 26 August.

1978 Retires from Boston University and returns to East Hampton, New York.

1

The Man behind the Music

In the foothills outside Naples, Italy, lies the town of Gragnano, known primarily for its production of excellent wine. To the citizens who inhabited Gragnano during the nineteenth century, the name Dello Joio was quite well known. For three generations dating back at least to the year 1829, the position of organist in the village church was occupied by a member of the Dello Joio family. The last in this succession was Casimiro Dello Joio (1881–1963). The oldest of twelve children, Casimiro began his musical training at the conservatory in Naples when he was quite young. In addition to becoming an accomplished organist, he also learned to play the flute. By the time he was a teenager, Casimiro began to feel that spending the rest of his life in Gragnano would not be very fulfilling, and he became restless. The opportunity to expand his horizons came when ships of the United States fleet docked in Naples for several days. The flagship commander carried a band on his ship that was short on personnel. Upon hearing that the United States Navy was recruiting members for the band, Casimiro auditioned and was accepted as a flutist. He signed on for a three year enlistment, at the end of which he was automatically awarded United States citizenship.

Upon his arrival in the United States at the end of his Naval service, Casimiro settled first in Pittsburgh where he took a job as organist in a hotel dining room. It was there that he became good friends with Victor Herbert who was conductor of the Pittsburgh Symphony from 1898–1904. Casimiro later moved to New York where he became organist at Our Lady of Mount Carmel Church in New York City. He also gave private lessons on the organ and piano. One of the students who came to study piano with him was a young lady by the name of Antoinette Garramone (1890–1952) who was born in New York of Italian parentage.

1

Casimiro married Antoinette and on 24 January 1913 their only child, Norman Dello Joio, was born.

Continuing the family tradition, Casimiro began training Norman to play the keyboard when he was around four or five years old. Casimiro not only taught him to play the piano and organ; he took him through the entire Naples Conservatory curriculum, teaching him the rudiments of theory, sight singing, and ear training. Norman described his father as "a very rigorous teacher—very demanding. I used to be terrified of him when I had to take a lesson."[1] Another aspect of Norman's training with his father, one that was to prove very valuable to him in his professional career, was their habit of sitting down every day and playing four-hand piano music. They played four-hand arrangements of the standard symphonic works such as those of Mozart, Beethoven, and Tchaikovsky. They also touched on some of the modern composers. Norman remembers particularly playing through the score of Stravinsky's *Petrouchka*. That work must have made a profound impression on him, for the famous "Petrouchka chord" (an F-sharp major arpeggio over a C major arpeggio that Stravinsky used to represent the simultaneous human and inanimate qualities of the puppet) figures prominently in many of Norman's mature works.

Although Casimiro composed several masses and lesser religious works during his lifetime, composition was not the primary motivating force in his life, nor did he intend that it should be for Norman. He later expressed dismay when his son decided to make composition his life's work. He was sure it would be a disaster financially. He was grooming Norman for a career in the organ loft; the occupation the Dello Joio men had pursued for a hundred years—it was the old European family tradition of passing the trade from father to son. Norman therefore spent a good portion of his youth assisting his father in his duties as organist in the Roman Catholic Church. At the age of twelve, Norman took his first professional position as organist/choirmaster at the Star of the Sea Church on City Island. He recalls the look of astonishment on the faces of the adult choir members as they listened to this precocious lad on the organ bench telling them what they were doing wrong and how terribly they were singing. He held that position until 1934, when he became organist/choirmaster at Saint Ann's Church in New York City, where he served until 1940. By that time he had decided that he had aspirations for a more glamourous career than that of a church musician confined to the organ loft. He resigned his position, thus ending a family tradition that had lasted well over one hundred years. Even though he would never again return to the organ loft in any official capacity, Norman maintains that the organ is still his favorite instrument to play. His experience in the church, particularly the knowledge of Gregorian Chant[2] that he acquired, made a lasting impression on him that would later manifest itself in his compositional style—a style that is frequently based on Gregorian themes and often reflects the smooth, linear quality of liturgical chant.

Casimiro was also responsible for enmeshing Norman in another centuries-old Italian tradition—opera. In addition to his duties at the church, Casimiro served as a coach for the Metropolitan Opera. Singers regularly visited the Dello Joio home for coaching, and as a child, Norman spent many nights lying in bed listening to the strains of Mozart, Verdi, and Puccini until the early hours of the morning. Even though he was born in New York, Norman could not escape his Italian heritage, and the influence of this melodic tradition is one of the prime reasons that he has come to be known as a "lyricist." On the CBS television program "Profile of a Composer," which aired in 1958, he described the tradition of the San Gennaro Festival which takes place annually in the section of New York called Little Italy. It is there where street musicians perform excerpts from famous operas.

Music is the Neapolitan national sport. I grew up near Little Italy, and the melodic tradition of this kind of music is inescapable for me. . . . Opera, to the Italians, is what Jazz is to the Americans. Something that surrounds them all their lives. A formal, complicated art whose slightest variation from tradition is noted even by children, traffic cops, and shoemakers. . . . To the Italians, the form is natural . . . because they have grown up with this music surrounding them. . . . To the poorest Italian in New York, something would be lacking without opera at the San Gennaro Festival.[3]

Throughout his life, Norman has had strong ties to the Italian operatic tradition. He likes to recall an incident that occured in 1939, when he visited Italy with his parents. He returned to the church in Gragnano where his forefathers had been organists for generations. After hearing him play the organ, the pastor of the church took him to the sacristy and pulled an old mildewed program out of the files. On the front page was the name of Norman's great grandfather who, as organist of the church, was acting as host to a visiting artist who was to give an organ recital. The organist's name was Vincenzo Bellini. The date was 1829. Norman has stated, "If my father had remained in Italy, I probably would have become an Italian opera composer in the tradition of Bellini, Donizetti, and Verdi."[4]

Norman's early experiences with religious music and Italian opera were to play a decisive role in his development as a composer. However, he did not spend his entire youth cloistered in the church, in the opera house, or at home practicing his music. He attended public school at P. S. 186 in New York City through the eighth grade. He attended high school at the All Hallows Institute, an experience he described as "a time of excruciating boredom."[5] He graduated from high school on 6 June 1930 at the age of seventeen. For a youngster growing up in New York during the decade of the 1920s, the influence of popular music was bound to have an effect. Jazz, Tin Pan Alley, and the music of Gershwin were all part of the exuberant, chaotic urban environment in which Norman grew up. He responded in particular to the animated, bouncing rhythm of jazz. As a teenager he began playing in dance bands for high school proms and private parties around the city. He eventually formed his own group, and the money he made from "jobbing around" was an important source of income for him and his parents during the years of the Great Depression. Even though he has never composed popular music, the spirit of popular music is often evident in his scores. An interesting amalgamation of musical traditions results when he combines the dynamic rhythmic of jazz dance with music that is melodically based on a liturgical theme (see the third movement of *Variations, Chaconne, and Finale*).

Yet another aspect of Norman's childhood that proved to be an important influence on his development was the informal education he received on the streets of New York. The formulation of his philosophy concerning the role of the musician in society (to be discussed later in this chapter) has its roots in these early childhood experiences. He described the situation as follows.

I was fortunate in having a musician for a father. Yet it did have its drawbacks, for I was daily confronted with the unsettling problem of growing up in a social environment that subscribed to values which seemed at variance with what I experienced at home. Things were different on the outside, for the making of human relationships came into being also on the streets of New York. It was no easy matter for me to prove to my gang of musically illiterate friends that I was not some effete odd ball. It took some time for me to come to the realization that Palestrina and Rossini were not household names, and these heroes of mine were more likely to be thought of by my friends as something out of a cookbook. I like to think I finally licked this problem to an extent, by an exercise of sheer will, for with grim determination on the baseball field, I made myself play better than they did.

However, juxtaposed to this I remember once when in high elation I rushed home to excitedly announce that the Babe—that is Babe Ruth—had hit a home run. I remember the anguish I felt at the blank, uncomprehending stares that greeted this momentous news. My father's ignorance was exposed. "Babe Ruth," he would ask, "Who's he?" Now obviously I was living in two different worlds. Yet there can be no doubt that they both had a profound influence on my life. I surmise that at that time I began to dimly perceive that in the process of seeking an identity, that between my home and the external world there had to be some common link. Finding its meaning would be something that I would ultimately have to discover for myself.[6]

The process of discovering that common link between his home and the external world led Norman to reach one important conclusion that would have a direct bearing on the music he composed. He maintains that "the more a composer lives in the world around him, the more his music reflects his world."[7] His music not only reflects the influence of the church, the opera house, and the popular music of his day; it also reflects that external world—a world which superficially is unrelated to music, but which to a sensitive, imaginative person like Norman yielded an abundance of musical ideas. Imagine, if you will, a scene on West 96th Street in New York City during the 1920s. Norman is inside dutifully practicing his music. A group of kids in the neighborhood is forming a ball team, and one of them begins banging his bat on the sidewalk in front of Norman's house and yelling, "Hey Norman! Hey Norman!" The sounds of that yell constitute a kind of universal call that every kid knows. The two syllables of the name Norman are chanted to the interval of a descending minor third. Set to music it would look something like this:

Example 1.

Nor - man

As you will discover in reading the subsequent chapters in which Dello Joio's music is discussed, the interval of the minor third plays a strategic role in the melodies of many of his important works. *The Triumph of Saint Joan, New York Profiles,* and *Song of the Open Road* are just a few notable examples.

Relating the use of the minor third in works Dello Joio composed as an adult to the childhood experience of hearing a street call is not mere speculation. On the television program "Profile of a Composer," he described this experience and then used an excerpt from one of his scores to show how that "universal call" is reflected in the music. On that same program he used the experience of a baseball game to demonstrate the multiplicity of rhythms that are a part of everyday life. The motion of the pitcher going through his windup, the catcher pounding his mitt, the infielders yelling such epithets as "This guy can't hit," while the crowd chants "We want a homer"—all of this going on simultaneously creates a very complex polyrhythm that would naturally be reflected in the music of a composer who is sensitive to the sounds of the world around him. Anyone listening to Dello Joio's music will immediately become aware that particularly in the fast movements, cross accents and polyrhythms abound. It is not a matter of the composer consciously imitating the sounds of the world around him, but as he put it, ". . . it always seemed obvious to me that rhythms come out of natural sources. A kid calling 'Hey Norman!' and the beating of my heart: these are certainly natural sources. Nothing mystical about them. I take my music from the sounds I hear around me, or feel within me. These influences are really minor. I don't consciously think of them when I write music. . . . They (musical ideas) come to mind freely and easily when I work."[8]

To describe Norman Dello Joio as precocious is an accurate assessment as far as his talents as a performer. However, as a composer, he was, relatively speaking, a late bloomer. He was almost twenty-five years old before he began to think seriously of making composition his life's work. The years immediately after graduation from high school (1930–33) were very unsettling for him. He was offered a scholarship to a college in Connecticut, but he turned it down. These were the worst years of the Depression. His father had lost his life savings when the stock market fell in 1929, and it was necessary for Norman to work in order to keep food on the family table. He continued his work as a church organist, and kept his dance band going. However, as any free-lance musician knows, playing in a dance band does not always provide a steady income. In 1931, Dello Joio's band was fired by the manager of a night club in Pittsburgh. The public didn't like their music, the manager didn't like it, and even Dello Joio admitted that it was pretty lousy. He attributed the problem to a drummer who couldn't keep a smidgen of rhythm.

During the school year he took a few courses at City College—math, economics, history—but not with any particular career in mind. It was just something to do. In the summers he pursued that other passion of his youth—baseball. As the second baseman for a semiprofessional team in the Twilight League in New York City, he received five dollars a game. A number of sources have alleged that Norman was offered a contract by a professional team. That is a slight exaggeration. A scout from the

New York Giants happened to be in the stands one day when Norman had a particularly good game. He managed four hits in four times at bat. After the game the scout approached him and asked if he would like to come down the following spring for a tryout with their Jersey City farm club. Norman was flattered by the offer, but he had serious doubts about his ability to ever reach the major leagues, and he rejected the offer. Still he has always maintained an intense interest in the game of baseball. In 1954, he was made an Honorary Life Member of the Association of Professional Baseball Players.

Still another opportunity presented Norman with a problem during these years. The head pastor at his father's church was a wealthy Italian Monsignor who was very conscious of Norman's talents. He offered to sponsor Norman if he would take his vows and go to Rome to train under Don Lorenzo Perosi who at that time occupied a position equivalent to that held by Palestrina in the sixteenth century. The Monsignor envisioned Norman returning to New York following his period of training and becoming his modern day Palestrina. But, the idea of taking vows and being a church composer the rest of his life did not appeal to Norman. He was already growing impatient with his position as a church organist. This, combined with the fact that he was coming to his own conclusions about what belief was (he never became a nonbeliever, but the firmness of his conviction lapsed somewhat) caused him to politely reject the Monsignor's offer.

It was also during this period that Norman's parents separated. The experience proved to be so emotionally devastating for his mother that she attempted suicide. Although his father had seen to his professional needs over the years, Norman had much stronger emotional ties to his mother. He described his father as outwardly friendly, fun-loving, and gregarious, but inwardly a severe, strict disciplinarian. His mother, on the other hand, was a warm, loving person who, having no career of her own, devoted her energies to the provision of her son's physical and emotional needs. His mother's suicide attempt was very upsetting for Norman who naturally felt a certain responsibility for her during the period of separation from his father. Casimiro's sense of responsibility was heightened by the life-threatening experience, and he and Antoinette ended their estrangement after a period of just over a year.

In 1933, after Norman finally decided to pursue a career in music, he accepted a scholarship from the Institute of Musical Art (later merged with the Juilliard Graduate School to become the Juilliard School of Music) and enrolled as an organ student of the Belgian organist, Gaston-Marie

Déthier. At the age of fifteen, Norman had begun studying organ with his Godfather, Pietro Yon, organist at St. Patrick's Cathedral. Yon had also instructed him in theory, and because of his prior theoretical studies, Norman was placed in the advanced theory class at the institute. It was during the course of his theoretical studies that he became intrigued by the process of putting notes together. When assignments were given in harmony and counterpoint, he would always produce more than what was required, and he began to formulate in his mind the idea of shifting his emphasis from performance to composition. After completing the requirements for the regular course in organ and receiving his diploma in May of 1936, he decided to apply to Juilliard as a composition student. He took a year off (1936–37) in order to compose the works that would be required for acceptance. It was during this period that he wrote his earliest compositions—a sonata for cello and piano, a song for voice and piano entitled *The Ballad of Thomas Jefferson*, a trio for violin, cello, and piano, a quartet for four bassoons, and a sonata for violin and piano. Except for the song, which was published, the scores of these works are lost.

Norman was accepted as a scholarship student at Juilliard and began his studies in composition there in the fall of 1937. His composition teacher was the teacher with whom he had studied theory as an undergraduate, Bernard Wagenaar. Norman completed the practical course in composition and received his diploma in May of 1939. He then enrolled in the Juilliard Graduate School and continued his studies in composition there until 1941. It was during the summer of 1941 that he met and studied composition with Paul Hindemith at the Berkshire Music Center at Tanglewood in Lenox, Massachusetts. Hindemith's composition class that summer included two other young composers who have become prominent on the American musical scene—Lukas Foss and Harold Shapero. During the following year (1941–42) Norman commuted to Yale University once a week to pursue his studies with Hindemith while at the same time continuing his studies with Wagenaar at Juilliard.

It is the opinion of Dello Joio scholars and Dello Joio himself that of his two composition teachers, Hindemith had the strongest, most lasting influence. Robert Sabin wrote: "The major external influence on his music has been . . . Paul Hindemith. . . . His studies with Hindemith . . . constituted a turning point in his life. Until that time, he had never fully realized what the challenges of contemporary music meant to his own development. The modernism of thought and method to which he was constantly exposed, the rigorous craftsmanship he was compelled to master had a tremendous impact upon him, more even than he was perhaps aware."[9] Nevertheless, the influence of Wagenaar should not be totally discounted. The following description of Wagenaar's music could in many respects be an accurate description of Dello Joio's music.

Wagenaar was able to arrive at his goal deriving what he needed from jazz or neoclassicism. . . . The excerpt shows the very lyrical nature of his music, with emphasis on the surge of melodic line. . . . His orchestration was influenced by Mahler, his harmony classified as French using a free chromaticism over a solid diatonic base, frequent first inversion triads, first or second inversions of sevenths moving freely to other such inversions from a different key; juxtaposition of two triads; dissonant clashes. . . . Characteristic are the building up of a highly organized structure from several short motives, the motorized use of fast passages, the constantly alive orchestration.[10]

From this description, it is apparent that even though Dello Joio was studying composition with two different teachers simultaneously, their basic philosophy and approach to music was at least compatible. Both Hindemith and Wagenaar espoused the principles of tonality as opposed to atonality, diatonicism as opposed to serialism, and music that was accessible as opposed to unapproachable by a wide general audience—all principles that Dello Joio has adhered to throughout his career.

At this point it would be well to briefly summarize the major trends in twentieth century music that were at work in the late 1930s and early 1940s that would likely have confronted Dello Joio in the early stages of his development as a composer.

During the late nineteenth and early twentieth centuries, it was fashionable for American musicians to go to Germany for musical study. Composers such as Edward MacDowell and Horatio Parker returned to the United States composing in a pseudo-Romantic style similar to that of Franz Liszt. World War I brought an abrupt halt to that trend. Following the war, American composers went to France for their training. During the decade following World War I, Arnold Schoenberg led the members of the Austro-German School from the ultra-chromatic world of Wagner into the realm of atonality and serialism. Simultaneously in France, where there had been a long-standing tradition of reacting negatively to anything Germanic, the Franco-Russian School led by Igor Stravinsky reacted to Schoenberg by moving into the neoclassical tradition. Neoclassicism implies "an objective, detached musical style that depends on a diatonic idiom—an idiom based on the seven note scale"[11] as opposed to the serialistic approach of giving equal importance to all twelve notes in the chromatic scale. Thus by the second decade of the twentieth century, European music was basically divided into two camps—the serialists or dodecaphonists led by Schoenberg, and the neoclassicists led by Stravinsky. From 1920 until 1950, the school that had the most far-reaching influence in the United States was the neoclassical school. Stravinsky was championed by Nadia Boulanger, a composition teacher in Paris whose widespread influence on American music in this century is well documented. Aaron Copland, Roy Harris, Samuel Barber, Virgil Thomson, Walter Piston, and Marc Blitzstein were among the famous American composers who studied with Boulanger. As Joan Peyser wrote in her book *The New Music*, "their accessible melodic music, unencumbered by harsh dissonance, drowned out dodecaphony in the United States. The Boulanger school had its counterparts in New England: Harold Shapero, Irving Fine, and Arthur Berger taught at Harvard where Leonard Bernstein was a student. At Tanglewood . . . Aaron Copland led the 'neo-classical school,' and Howard Hanson was director of the Eastman School of Music in Rochester, New York. Vladimir Ussachevsky has said that a student at Eastman could not hear any Schoenberg, Webern, or Berg during the late thirties and early forties."[12]

During the 1920s, the International Composers Guild (ICG), led by experimentalist Edgard Varèse, sponsored a series of concerts in New York that included first performances of many modern composers, including Schoenberg, Webern, and of course many of Varèse's own works. Varèse's experiments with volumes and densities of sound as opposed to conventional harmonies and melodies led eventually to the modern day phenomenon of electronic music. The ICG was short-lived, however, and by 1927, "neo-classicism . . . promulgated through the recently formed League of Composers, triumphed over Varèse and his advanced musical colleagues."[13] Varèse returned to Paris, and from then until the late forties, experimental music in the United States was centered on the West Coast with composers such as John Cage and Harry Partch.

From this brief sketch, it should be clear that the musical environment to which Dello Joio was exposed as a young composer was a conservative one that had its roots in the diatonic, tonally based music of the neoclassical school. Add to this the more direct influence of Hindemith who in *The Craft of Musical Composition*, published in two volumes in 1937 and 1939, dismissed atonality and polytonality as "outmoded ideas, contrary to psychological and acoustical fact,"[14] and declared that "the tone row destroyed the gravitational uprightness of traditional harmony,"[15] and it is easy to understand why serialism and atonality never appeared in Dello Joio's music until the 1960s when he, like Stravinsky in the 1950s, adapted the twelve-tone method to his own personal idiom. In Dello Joio's case this is confined to only four works. He has not adopted serialism exclusively during his later years.

From the very beginning then, Dello Joio's music, although at times written in a wild, carefree manner that Hindemith would tame, had a strong melodic appeal, clearly defined formal structure, and a strong diatonic base, even though the melody and harmony derived material freely from all twelve notes. Once he began to compose in earnest, he wrote prolifically as though he were making up for lost time. It was not long before his talents were recognized. His piano trio won the Elizabeth Sprague Coolidge Award in 1937. The *Magnificat* for orchestra won the Town Hall Composition Award in 1943, and was nominated along with Leonard Bernstein's *Jeremiah* Symphony and William Schuman's Symphony no. 5 for the Critic's Circle Award for that year. Dello Joio became eagerly sought after by the leading performers of the period. His first piano sonata was written for Sidney Foster, *Trio* for flute, cello, and piano for the LeRoy, Foster, Scholz Trio, and *The Mystic Trumpeter* for Robert Shaw and the Collegiate Chorale.

With his career as a composer launched, Dello Joio made another decision in the early forties that would be of lasting significance. Having resigned his position as a church organist in 1940, he became musical director for Eugene Loring's Dance Players from 1941–43. This was the beginning of a long and very satisfying relationship between Dello Joio and the world of dance. Loring had heard Dello Joio's *Sinfonietta* for orchestra performed at Juilliard and thought that it had possibilities for a ballet. Dello Joio made a two piano arrangement which was used for the ballet *Prairie* based on the poem by Carl Sandburg. Dello Joio also wrote *The Duke of Sacramento* for Loring's group, which premiered it in October of 1942 at the Phillips-Mill Playhouse in New Jersey. In 1944, he was commissioned by Boston's Ballet Theatre to write *On Stage*, which became one of their most popular repertory pieces and was toured in both the United States and England. In 1948, Dello Joio's work attracted the attention of Martha Graham, and he wrote the first of four ballets for her—*Diversion of Angels* (originally titled *Wilderness Stair*, the music is the same as the *Serenade* for orchestra). The other three are *Seraphic Dialogue* (performed to the music of the *Triumph of Saint Joan Symphony*), *Time of Snow* (more often heard in a transcription for band titled *Heloise and Abelard*), and *Exaltation of Larks* (1978) which due to unfortunate circumstances was never performed. Dello Joio's Pulitzer Prize-winning composition, *Meditations on Ecclesiastes*, was originally written as the ballet *There Is a Time*, which José Limòn choreographed for Juilliard's American Music Festival in April of 1956. Dello Joio expressed the philosophy behind his approach to writing music for dance in an article that appeared in *Dance Perspectives in 1963*.

> Music and dance are allied arts. Dance may not be a lesser art, but it has no life of its own disassociated from music. It derives its stimulus from music. I am aware that some people hold the opposite point of view—that the music should be inspired by the dance for which it is written. As a composer, I take exception to this. Though it is possible for a composer to write this way, I doubt that the resultant score can have very much musical merit.
>
> In composing for dance, as in composing for concert performance, I strive to shape a cohesive piece of music based on an underlying thematic principle. I dislike the type of music that fills in background or marks time in order for the dancer to make the necessary steps. . . . In my opinion the choreographer should try to capture the emotional essence of the music rather than confining his attention to its technical structure.[16]

With such a philosophy behind them, it is not surprising that Dello Joio's ballet scores were either originally written as abstract music and later adapted for ballet, or have become popular as concert works apart from the stage. For that reason the dance music is discussed in subsequent chapters dealing with his concert music rather than in a separate chapter devoted to music for dance.

It was in 1940 that Dello Joio met Grayce Baumgold, the daughter of a New York diamond broker. The two were introduced at a musicale at which some of Dello Joio's music was performed. Miss Baumgold was an amateur ballet dancer, and for the next two years she and Norman attended ballet, concert, and opera performances together. With World War II raging in Europe and the Pacific, Norman expected to be drafted and sent overseas so he and Grayce were married on 5 June 1942. Their marriage produced three children—Victoria (b. 1952), Justin (b. 1954), and Norman Adrian (b. 1956). Justin is now a composer in his own right, assuring that the Dello Joio musical tradition will continue for at least one more generation. Norman's marriage to Grayce ended in divorce in 1971.

As fate would have it, Norman was exempted from military service because of a heart murmur and remained in the United States for the duration of the war. Two Guggenheim Fellowships in 1944 and 1945, and a one thousand dollar grant from the American Academy of Arts and Letters enabled him to devote most of his time to composition during those years. He used that time to polish his skills. Hindemith had taught him to look upon composing as a craft that required discipline and concentrated effort to master. Simply being modern would not provide sufficient cover for bad technique and unclear formulation. Just as the performer must practice his instrument every day, so the composer must practice composition. As a result, Dello Joio developed a habit that he has maintained throughout his career—that of getting up at dawn every morning and spending his first four to five waking hours composing. No amount of procrastination or lack of inspiration is allowed to prevent that.

From 1943 on, Dello Joio was no longer under the watchful eye of his composition teachers. He was on his own. The works composed during the years 1943–45 show him moving out of the derivative stage and developing his own musical personality. Works such as the Second Piano Sonata, *Concert Music* for orchestra, and the *Trio* for flute, cello, and piano reveal a kind of probing search into the problems of development and manipulation of thematic material. In *Concert Music*, the use of a four-note motto, which recurs throughout the work as a unifying motive, is the first step in a process that leads to the use of thematic cells as building blocks in his more mature works. With the Concerto for harp and orchestra he made his first excursion into the variations form, a form that has continued to serve him well throughout his career.

In 1945, with the term of his second Guggenheim Fellowship expired and the income from his music not yet providing a sufficient sum for he and his wife to live on, Dello Joio accepted a position as teacher of composition at Sarah Lawrence College in Bronxville, New York. He succeeded William Schuman who left to become director of the Juilliard School of Music. The contract called for him to teach two days a week. In addition to composition, he taught a course on materials of music for the general student. It was not the typical music appreciation course that most college students take as a part of the liberal education requirement. Dello Joio actually had these students involved in the creative task of composing music. As a result of this experience he formulated some significant ideas on the role of music in education which he expressed in an unpublished article entitled "Music in Education."

My approach to education is through music, because that is the way I became educated. Everything else but music was merely an accompaniment to the central part of my life. But it was music which taught me about personal standards of honesty, integrity, craftsmanship, scholarship, and taught me to love the work of artists and of honest men, whether in literature, politics, education, or music. I think that those people who like music and like to hear it, play it, or compose it should study it as a central part of their education in school or in college. This is because . . . it is an important way for people to become educated. The prime reason for teaching any art is to establish an attitude towards contemporary life, one that not only assimilates, but also rejects. It is possible for students who have no talent for music (as composers or performers) to gain an intelligent understanding of music, and to gain insight into the implications of the subject matter for contemporary culture. Thus they will learn to counteract the questionable and supplement the desirable practices that have shaped and are making our musical world.

Although teaching never became more than a part-time activity for Dello Joio, he has always maintained close ties with the educational system in this country through frequent lectures and appearances as guest composer on college campuses and in the public schools. This relationship later bore tangible fruit through his activities with the Ford Foundation Contemporary Music Project, of which more will be said later.

During Dello Joio's five year tenure at Sarah Lawrence composition continued to be the central focus of his life. The long years of training and rigorous discipline to which he had subjected himself began to pay off. His music now revealed the confident work of a mature artist and began to attract the attention of the nation's leading conductors. Fritz Reiner performed *Concert Music* with the Pittsburgh Symphony in January of 1946. In December of that year Dello Joio appeared as soloist in his own *Tre Ricercare* for piano and orchestra with George Szell and the New York Philharmonic. Reiner and the Pittsburgh Symphony also gave the premier of *Variations, Chaconne, and Finale* (the work premiered under the title *Three Symphonic Dances*) in January of 1948, and Bruno Walter gave the New York premiere of the same work the following December. That performance gained Dello Joio the New York Music Critics Circle Award for the outstanding new orchestral work of the 1948–49 season.

The year 1946 also brought Dello Joio the first opportunity for recognition outside the United States. The Polish Counsul General in New York had heard Dello Joio perform the *Tre Ricercare*, and asked him if he would be interested in making a concert tour of Poland. Dello Joio accepted, and in December 1946, he and conductor Franco Autori toured Cracow, Lodz, Katowice, Sopot, Gdánsk, and Warsaw with a program of American music that included Copland's *Rodeo Suite*, Barber's *Adagio for Strings*, and Dello Joio's *Tre Ricercare*. The critics from the Polish newspapers consistently proclaimed Dello Joio's work as the most interesting of the three works presented.

Dello Joio was also active in the League of Composers during this time, and in that capacity actively promoted the performance of new music. Early in 1946, he outlined to the league a plan to bring contemporary composers and performers of serious music together for the purpose of making each other aware of their common interests and problems. He saw to it that invitations were issued to pianists who were before the public to attend a meeting in a private home at which certain composers would be assembled to present their own music. Present at the meeting were seven composers whose works had been screened from a large number of compositions by a committee from the league. Seventy-five pianists attended the initial meeting which featured an informal, free exchange of ideas. As a result, three compositions were chosen by pianists for their programs that season.

By the late forties, Dello Joio had gained recognition as one of the nation's leading composers. From that time on, commissions and contracts for new compositions came about as fast as he could fulfill them. For example, the famous jazz clarinetist Artie Shaw heard one of Dello Joio's compositions performed at Carnegie Hall, went backstage and commissioned him on the spot to write the Concertante for clarinet and orchestra. Shaw premiered the work on 22 May 1949. That composition, along with Stravinsky's *Ebony Concerto* written for Woody Herman and Copland's Concerto for clarinet and orchestra written for Benny Goodman, has been cited as one of the three principal works written in that medium since World War II. [17]

Having gained an international reputation, Dello Joio resigned his position at Sarah Lawrence in 1950 in order to devote full time to composition. Since that time he has been one of only a half-dozen American composers of serious music who has been able to live solely off the commissions and royalties from the sale and performance of his music. The vast majority of American composers in this century have had to hold teaching positions in colleges and universities or have some other source of income in order to exist outside of abject poverty. Why has Dello Joio been able to achieve success when so many others could not? There are several reasons. First of all, his systematic, disciplined approach to composition enabled him to develop his craft to the point that he has always been able to turn out a quality product on demand. Those who commissioned Dello Joio knew that he would write a good composition that was guaranteed to have an appeal to performer and audience alike. The second reason is that Dello Joio writes music that is accessible to a broad cross section of the general public, not music which Roger Sessions described as "art for the initiated, art too complex for the bourgeoise."[18] Taking his stimulus from Hindemith who endorsed the Gebrauchmusik (functional music) idea and avowed his commitment to music for everyone, Dello Joio has always maintained the hope that his music would be heard and accepted by the general public. He has often expressed his concern for the gap that exists between the composer of serious music and the general public, and stated that "the composer who shrugs this off does so at his own peril."[19]

The third reason for Dello Joio's success is that he has never felt it disdainful to write for amateurs, and his music has gained wide acceptance among the many performing organizations in the nation's secondary schools, colleges, and universities. As his career advanced, he found himself working at many levels: television, the theatre and opera, ballet, and music for the school and the church. All of these worlds became creative outlets and each in its own way afforded him the opportunity to reach a wide segment of society. He reached certain conclusions about the function of music in society which he revealed in a lecture at Boston University.

. . . What did loom large in my mind was that no matter why I did it (wrote music), it ultimately involved others, and that music making . . . had an ethical purpose. Increasingly an awareness manifested itself that music had within it the power to bring human beings together to share in common a harmonious purpose. I am not necessarily talking about what we think of as so-called high art. We should separate the use of music as exemplified by the glamorous virtuoso or conductor and that of a school chorus or elementary band or amateur quartet. To those involved in what we consider music making at a less than high professional standard this seems to suggest that it is in the nonprofessional and his efforts that the true spirit of music lies, for he brings to music a pure love of the art itself without ego concerns. . . . I must admit to being as moved at a group of unformed voices singing a universal theme of love by Walt Whitman as I am at a highly professional organization projecting Beethoven's thought, "Be Embraced, Ye Millions."[20]

Even though Dello Joio has continued to write for professional organizations and individuals throughout his career, a substantial number of his commissions have involved writing for amateur performing organizations in schools and churches across the country.

During the 1950s, Dello Joio's star continued to rise. In 1957 he was awarded an Honorary Doctor of Music degree from Lawrence University in Appleton, Wisconsin, an honor that has since been bestowed on him by the University of Cincinnati, Saint Mary's College, and Colby College. He was awarded the Pulitzer Prize for music in 1957, and in 1958 he was featured in a one hour CBS television program, "Profile of a Composer." He won his second New York Music Critics Circle Award in 1959, for his opera *The Triumph of Saint Joan.*

The circumstances surrounding the composition of *Meditations on Ecclesiastes*, for which Dello Joio won the Pulitzer Prize, warrant discussion in some detail because they provide significant insight into his creative process. In March of 1955, William Schuman commissioned Dello Joio to write a ballet score for José Limòn to choreograph for Juilliard's American Music Festival in April of 1956. Early in 1956, as the deadline approached for completion of the ballet score, Dello Joio was also under contract with CBS television to write the background music for over twenty films to be used in their forthcoming series, "Air Power." He described the process of working under constant pressure to meet deadlines.

I was writing against deadlines to get the music ready for the "Air Power" series to record. I would go down to CBS every afternoon to do my writing. I had an office down there with a movie projector to run the film so that I could see what had to be done musically to cover the things that were all prearranged with the director. . . . It was all cut and arranged to the split second, so I just had to write, which was a totally different thing from what I was doing in the mornings. Before I would go down to CBS, I worked on the ballet *There Is a Time*, which was a totally different kind of creative process. This went on for about six months. . . . I just delivered the music for *There Is a Time* to Limòn . . . and never saw him. I never went to rehearsals. He just took the music and started choreographing. I'll never forget the experience when I went to the opening of the ballet. I actually had no recollection of what I had done. I had no idea what was going to happen musically. I was sitting there as though someone else had written it. . . . Usually when I write something I'm into it so deeply that I know every note, every rest, everything about the piece . . . but this was one of those strange kind of circumstances where I was so involved with a large project such as "Air Power" that I had no alternative but to write. Obviously while I was writing I was very concentrated on what I was doing as far as the ballet was concerned, but when I'd go down town to the other I had to change gears so completely into a different kind of thing. I was operating in two different worlds creatively, one having nothing to do with the other.[21]

It is significant that *Meditations on Ecclesiastes* (concert title of *There Is a Time*), one of Dello Joio's finest works, the one that brought him his most significant award, was composed under conditions of extreme pressure. There was no time to reflect on what he had done and possibly try alternative solutions to compositional problems. It was a severe test of endurance during which Dello Joio's mind must have been taxed to the limit. The fact that he was unable to recall what he had written at the time of the work's first performance is an indication that he may have been working in an altered state of consciousness brought on by anxiety and nervous exhaustion. The true nature of the creative process is something we are only beginning to understand, and perhaps this example will shed some light on the subject.

The period from 1950 to the early sixties was a period in which Dello Joio became heavily involved in the field of dramatic music. During the previous decade he wrote nothing for stage or screen except for three ballet scores and a documentary film score, *Greentree Thoroughbred*. Most of his efforts during that period were concentrated on orchestral music, keyboard music, chamber music, and vocal music for either chorus or solo voice. It would be a slap in the face of tradition if a composer with Dello Joio's Italian heritage did not compose an opera, and true to that tradition, his first opera, *The Triumph of Joan*, was produced in 1950. It was later completely revised for an NBC television production in 1956, and given a new title—*The Trial at Rouen*. For the 1959 stage production by the New York City Opera Company, the title was changed again to *The Triumph of Saint Joan*. In 1953–54, Dello Joio wrote his second opera, *The Ruby*. His third opera, *Blood Moon*, was composed during the years 1959–61. (For a thorough discussion of all of the operas, see chapter 9.) The success of the "Air Power" series brought Dello Joio additional contracts to write for television (*Here is New York, Vanity Fair, America and Americans, The Saintmaker's Christmas Eve, Time of Decision,* and *The Louvre*), and for a time during the late fifties he was actively working through an agent in California to obtain a contract for a Hollywood movie score. He also started a Broadway musical, but due to contractual difficulties never finished it. Two scores of incidental music— *The Tall Kentuckian* (1953) and *Anthony and Cleopatra* (1960)—also date from this period.

Although television opened up new creative vistas for Dello Joio and rewarded him handsomely for his efforts, the area in which he coveted success the most was opera. America had not produced a major opera composer up to that time (up to the present time for that matter), certainly no one of the stature that Verdi and Wagner achieved in the last century. With his lyric gift, his Italian heritage, and the financial assistance of the Ford Foundation which in 1959 announced a new program to underwrite the production costs of new American operas, perhaps there was a glimmer of hope for a composer like Dello Joio. *The Ruby* received favorable criticism when it premiered in 1955, *The Trial at Rouen* was a smashing success on nationwide television in 1956, and *The Triumph of Saint Joan* had received an award in 1959. The signs were encouraging. However, that glimmer of hope was squelched in 1961, when Dello Joio's first full-length opera—*Blood Moon*—met with a barrage of unfavorable criticism by the press. After having spent three years on the score, he was sorely disappointed with such an outcome and thoroughly disgusted with a good number of critics. The whole affair left him with such a poor aftertaste that he has not attempted another opera since, although he maintains that if he could get the rights to Hemingway's *For Whom the Bell Tolls*, he would start it immediately. In his mind the lack of suitable dramatic material, a scarcity of skilled librettists, and the economics of producing opera create almost insurmountable problems for the American opera composer.

At the same time that Dello Joio was at work on *Blood Moon*, he was embarking on a project that would give his creative efforts a new focus and have a substantial impact on the field of music education in America— the Ford Foundation Young Composer's Project. In April 1958, Dello Joio was invited by McNeil Lowry, head of the Ford Foundation Humanities and Arts Program, to participate in discussions about the Ford Foundation's plan to support creative artists. After an initial meeting with representatives from the visual arts, theatre, and music, Dello Joio was given a couple of days to think over ways in which the situation might be improved for the young composer. Reflecting back on his own career, he recalled that when he finished at Juilliard he had no place to go where he could earn a living composing music. He had to earn a living doing things that were peripheral to his main interest. It occurred to him that during his visits to MENC conventions, schools, and colleges on behalf of his publisher, the performing organizations he had heard were quite good. He therefore formulated the idea of placing young composers in a school where they would have no assignment other than writing music for the school's performing organizations. The plumber, the carpenter, and the electrician were paid to provide a service; why not pay a composer to practice his trade. He took the idea back to the panel at the Ford Foundation, and strangely, or perhaps predictably, the people who objected the most were his fellow composers. They felt that having to write down to the level of these amateur performing organizations would amount to artistic bondage. Dello Joio responded that as a young composer, he would have liked to have written knowing first of all that his music would be performed, and second that he would be getting paid for it rather than writing a master symphony that would likely never be played. He maintained that many good composers were writing functional music, and being functional did not make it bad. Mr. Lowry liked the idea of having school children exposed to a living composer in their own community rather than one out of the history books. As a result the Ford Foundation set aside $200,000 to fund the program for three years. The goal was to place twenty-five composers in secondary public school systems across the country. The program was administered by the National Music Council, and Dello Joio was appointed chairman of a national committee to aid in the selection of composers. The committee upheld the position that no particular style of composition would be fostered. Creative imagination and technical ability were the prime factors in a candidate's selection. Among the composers selected for this initial phase of the project were Grant Beglarian, who later became Dean of the School of Performing Arts at the University of Southern California, and Peter Schickele, who later achieved notoriety as an authority on the music of P. D. Q. Bach. The program was successful enough that the Ford Foundation extended it for two more years. During the first five years of operation, the Young Composers Project placed thirty-nine composers under thirty-five years of age in forty-four communities throughout the country. Nineteen of them received appointments for a second year that were funded by the local school system.

The most crucial problem faced by the young composers in the project was the fact that many of the music teachers in the schools were ill-equipped to deal with contemporary music. They had received their training in archaic systems where the harmony studied was roughly that of Bach through Brahms, and music history courses seldom ventured beyond Debussy. In order to remedy that situation, the title of the Young Composers Project was changed to Contemporary Music Project (CMP), and the scope was broadened to include three major points of focus: 1) Assignment of composers under thirty-five years of age to a year of residency in selected school systems; 2) Establishment of seminars and workshops on contemporary music and creativity in music education; and 3) Establishment of pilot projects at the elementary and secondary level in selected school systems to initiate methods of presenting contemporary music and encourage development and realization of creative talent.

The Ford Foundation awarded a six year grant of $1,300,000 to the MENC to begin with the 1964–65 school year. Dello Joio was appointed

Chairman of the Project Policy Committee for CMP, and served in that capacity until 1972, when he resigned to become Dean of the School of the Arts at Boston University. An additional grant of $1,380,000 supplemented by $100,000 from MENC enabled CMP to continue through 1974, when funding was stopped and the project terminated. During the fifteen year history of CMP, thirteen of which were administered by a policy committee headed by Dello Joio, some seventy-five composers were placed in selected school systems throughout the United States. All of the music written by these composers was collected and placed in a microfilm library. Much of it was published, adding significantly to the body of music available to performing organizations in the schools. Seminars and Institutes on Comprehensive Musicianship were organized which examined current practices in music education, and in many cases found them wanting. As a result, a number of teacher training institutions such as Ithaca College in New York and Wichita State University in Kansas redesigned their music curriculum in order to foster a more integrated, humanistic approach to the teaching of music in the schools. During the final phase of the project (1969–74) a supplement was added to the program. Composers, not necessarily young, were placed in residence in middle-sized communities that were likely to have some cultural resources such as dance, theatre, and musical groups for which composers could write. The cities chosen were Louisville, Wichita, Honolulu, Anchorage, Plymouth (Michigan), Tampa, Minneapolis, Boston, and Indianapolis. These projects were Dello Joio's answer to what he believed to be a split between professional groups and between the professional and educational worlds. "You'd be surprised," he said, "at the separation between cultural groups in a community. Dancers, for example, don't think of getting to know their local composers."[22] Since the termination of CMP, some aspects of its program, such as the practice of placing creative artists in residence, have been taken over by the National Endowment for the Arts and various state arts councils. The final result is that the Young Composers Project, an idea that originated with Dello Joio and expanded into CMP, has had, and will continue to have, a significant impact on the musical life of this country.

As a result of Dello Joio's involvement with CMP and its close alliance with MENC, he shifted the focus of his own creative activity. In 1963, he wrote his first composition for band—*Variants on a Medieval Tune*—and since that time, more than half of his compositions have been for performers in the educational sphere.

In addition to his activities with CMP, Dello Joio has been involved in various arts projects sponsored by the United States government. In 1958, he was invited by the United States Information Agency to tour Russia as a member of the first delegation of composers to go to the Soviet Union under the Cultural Exchange Agreement. Due to other commitments, he was unable to accept the invitation. However, he was involved when the Soviet Union reciprocated. In November of 1959, he hosted in his home a group of Soviet and American composers. Present were Copland, Schuman, Barber, Menin, Ulysses Kay, Nicolas Slonimsky (as interpreter), and Shastakovich, Kabalevsky, Tikhon, Krennikov, Kikret Amirov, Konstantin Dankevich, and a critic—Boris Yarustovsky. They discussed a number of issues, but at the heart of the discussion was the freedom of the composer to be bold and the limitations faced by the Soviet composers whose duty it is to write music that is immediately accessible to the millions. The Soviet's view was that Western Art has lost all impulse to communicate with all but a narrow, sophisticated clique, a view with which Dello Joio could be somewhat sympathetic. This should in no way be understood as an endorsement of the Soviet practice of censoring the nonconforming artist. As Dello Joio stated later, "If one begins to fund certain artists and art forms, they will be the ones whose work is safe and popular, and the nonconventional artists, unable to compete with subsidized work, will not survive."[23] Dello Joio did tour Russia, Rumania, and Bulgaria under the auspices of the State Department's Cultural Exchange Program from 12 November to 23 December 1964. He conducted performances of his music and met with committees of composers to exchange information.

In April of 1966, Dello Joio was the United States representative to the Festival of the Arts in this Century held in Hawaii. The festival was sponsored by the Center for Cultural Exchange between East and West, a project of the United States government and the University of Hawaii. Dello Joio and the Japanese composer Toshiro Mayazumi were the featured composers.

From 1963–65, Dello Joio served on the Research Advisory Council of the United States Office of Education. He quickly became discouraged with his work on that council because he believed that too often projects were funded on the basis of political decisions rather than artistic merit. As a result of the experience he has become very cautious in advocating government support of the arts. He is of the opinion that funds should be appropriated by Congress, but they should be administered by an independent organization free of interference from the elected officials of government.

In the summer of 1972, Dello Joio was invited by the administration of

Boston University to join the faculty of the School of the Arts. Having recently gone through the personal upheaval of a divorce, he felt that a change of scenery might be in order, and he accepted the offer. Not long after that, the school's dean, Edwin E. Stein, resigned to become president of the Minneapolis Society of Fine Arts. Dello Joio was asked if he would take on the dean's duties as well. He agreed with the understanding that he would not be expected to give up his creative activity. As a free-lance man, he was wary of the draining effect of institutional affiliation. Yet he accepted the professorship and deanship because be believed that he, as a creative man, could influence attitudes and establish policies to promote professionalism in ways an academician could not. He established three primary goals for the School of the Arts: 1) Prepare students in their chosen fields on a professional basis; 2) Train educators in the arts to bring to their teaching professional competencies as musicians, actors, and artists; 3) Get faculty and students more involved with other faculty and students outside their own discipline.

When Dello Joio was at Sarah Lawrence College twenty-five years earlier, he had observed the existence of rather provincial attitudes on the part of the students and faculty. There was no communication between dancers and musicians or musicians and actors. His solution to that problem was to write the opera *The Triumph of Joan* for student performance so that all of the students—musicians, actors, dancers, scene designers, technicians—had a common project that could bring them together to develop a common understanding of one another's problems. He found that attitudes at Boston University were no different. Therefore he developed a similar solution. He wrote incidental music for the play *Thezmorphoriasuzae* by Aristophanes, and the play was produced by the students and faculty in the School of the Arts. The results in both instances were the same. When placed in a situation where they were forced to communicate with one another, students overcame provincial barriers and prejudicial attitudes.

Even during these hectic years as a full-time administrator, Dello Joio never lost sight of what had always been the central focus of his career—composing music. By the time he arrived at the office around ten o'clock in the morning for his daily appointments, he had already spent three to four hours composing. As a matter of fact, these were quite prolific years for him. Between 1974 and 1976 alone, he wrote in addition to the incidental music just mentioned, two complete settings of the Mass, two extended works for band, two extended works for orchestra, a song cycle for baritone and orchestra, and a number of smaller works.

After his retirement from Boston University in 1978, Dello Joio moved back to his home in East Hampton, New York, where he resides with his present wife Barbara Bolton, a professional actress who he married in 1974. Now in his seventies, he is still quite energetic and leads an active life. Mornings are taken up with composing, afternoons with swimming or tennis, and evenings are for relaxation.

Although it is difficult to predict how future historians will assess Dello Joio's impact on the world of twentieth century American music, perhaps a summation of how he is viewed by some of his contemporaries will offer some insight. Among those composers who emerged during the forties and fifties, Dello Joio is consistently listed as one of the most significant. Describing the American musical scene at midpoint in the century, the *New Oxford History of Music* states: "Among the established composers, the most important appeared to be Copland, Barber, Piston, Shuman, Dello Joio, Thomson, Sessions, and Riegger; and Ives's reputation was rising."[24] William Schuman states that "in terms of craft, he (Dello Joio) belongs in the top category of American composers."[25] Grant Beglarian considers Dello Joio "an important contributor to the American musical scene." "His lasting significance is only a guess," states Beglarian, "but he is not easily dismissable. A significant number of his works should bring pleasure to future generations."[26]

Dello Joio is not without his critics, however, particularly among the younger generation of composers that emerged during the late fifties and sixties. By this time, "the influence of Schoenberg and Webern was beginning for the first time to be strongly felt and reflected by American composers, and Stravinsky's conversion to serialism prompted a further movement towards the international avant-garde style."[27] This style is reflected in the music of composers such as Karlheinz Stockhausen in Germany, Pierre Boulez in France, and Milton Babbit in the United States. The musical language spoken by these composers is rooted in dodecaphony and concerned with the total organization (serialization) of every factor of the composition—notes, rhythm, dynamics, texture, and instrumentation. Melody and rhythm in the traditional sense are pulverized and any hint of consonance is avoided. Composers such as Schuman, Barber, and Dello Joio suddenly found themselves in the backwash. Their simple, melodious, tonally based music was regarded as conservative by the members of this new generation who were interested "neither in simplicity nor Americanism."[28] Commenting on this trend, Schuman stated: "The younger generation of composers tends to dismiss the music of the immediately preceding generation. The younger composers who were emerging in the late fifties and early sixties espoused the twelve-tone system and more avant-garde styles of music. Dello Joio was suddenly old fashioned. This was true of other composers of his generation. Dello Joio has suffered because his music doesn't fit the notion of those who are currently responsible for programming. This is not because his music is not good, but it simply is not currently in vogue. This tendency is receding and a greater appreciation for the mainstream composers is now emerging."[29]

Dello Joio flirted briefly with serialism and avant-garde practices during the early sixties in works such as *Colloquies* for violin and piano. However, he found this aesthetic direction so antithetical to the manner of artistic expression that he had developed prior to that time and has continued since, that he rejected it out of hand and steadfastly refused to be influenced by the members of this younger generation and the vagaries of public opinion that formerly held him in high esteem and now suddenly regarded him as outdated. Because he refused to change with the times, it is not likely that future generations will regard him as a pioneer who blazed new trails in the art of composing, but rather as a true craftsman who thoroughly understands his art. In Beglarian's words, "In professional circles his (Dello Joio's) music is not studied for innovation and avant-garde practices, but rather for professional craftsmanship. . . . He has mastered all aspects of the craft of composing."[30]

In addition to the word "craftsman," the other term that appears most often among those who assess Dello Joio's music is "people's composer." Howard Hanson described the musical avant-garde as "a group of composers writing for each other or for a precious audience of one hundred."[31] Dello Joio is not concerned with writing for other composers or a sophisticated audience of connoisseurs, but for the public at large. He is people-oriented. He considers himself a working musician whose job it is to write pleasurable music that communicates immediately with the listener. While some consider this a weakness, others regard it as a strength. In a modern, diverse society that values freedom of artistic expression, there is bound to be diversity among those who express themselves through musical composition, and it is inevitable that the language of music will continue to change. Yet as long as there is a listening public that appreciates a well-crafted musical composition with a strong melodic vein that is easily comprehendible, Dello Joio's music will have a place.

2

Vocal Music

Although Dello Joio has composed in every genre of serious music, he has been most prolific in the field of vocal music. The choral works number forty-five separate titles, and there are twenty-five compositions for solo voice. This list does not include the operas because they are discussed in a separate chapter.

It is appropriate to begin the study of Dello Joio's music by looking first at the choral works. Because of the accessibility of his style, many of these compositions are performed frequently by high school and college choirs, and thus the average person is apt to be introduced to Dello Joio through his choral music. The works for solo voice will be discussed in the second half of this chapter.

The choral works range in conception from the large-scale, multi-movement *Symphony for Voices and Orchestra* to brief madrigal-like settings such as *Adieu, Mignonne, When You Are Gone.* All of the choral works require instrumental accompaniment of some kind. *The Mystic Trumpeter*, which calls for solo French horn, is the only work that approaches the a cappella medium. Probably because of the circumstances under which a given work is likely to be performed, the most frequently used accompanying instrument is the piano. However, when circumstances allowed, Dello Joio has shown an inclination toward the combination of brass instruments and choir. Most of the medium-length works call for either brass, brass and organ, brass and percussion, or brass and strings. The only works that require woodwind instruments are the large-scale works for choir and orchestra.

The vocal writing in Dello Joio's choral works demonstrates a thorough knowledge of the human voice and its capabilities. The individual voice parts are well conceived, and the dissonant harmonies are made less difficult to sing by the logic of the voice leading. Range and tessitura are always within acceptable limits. A homophonic texture which tends toward declamation is the norm. Examples of imitative polyphony can be found, but they are generally short-lived. Extended contrapuntal passages are more apt to be found in the accompaniment. The accompaniment functions independently of the voice parts, supporting them through thematic elaboration and tonal relationships. All of Dello Joio's vocal works reveal a composer who is keenly sensitive to the text. The musical elements are carefully calculated to enhance the sound, rhythm, and meaning of the poem as a whole and each individual phrase.

Dello Joio's choice of poets for his choral settings shows a broad acquaintance with the literature. He has confessed to being an avid reader of poetry. Discounting for the moment the sacred works, the majority of the poets whose works he has selected for musical setting are English and American poets of the nineteenth and twentieth centuries, and of these the overwhelming favorite is Walt Whitman. Dello Joio is not alone in his preference for Whitman. A recently completed doctoral dissertation entitled *The Musical Settings of Walt Whitman*[1] reveals that Whitman has been set to music by American composers more than any other writer. Shakespeare is the only writer of any competitive standing. Dello Joio's interest in Whitman spans a period of thirty-eight years, beginning with the setting of *Vigil Strange* in 1941, and ending with *As of a Dream*, a masque based on writings of Whitman completed in 1979. In the intervening years he set nine additional Whitman poems to music. Because of the significance of the Whitman settings they will be discussed as a group, followed by consideration of the remaining secular works, and concluding with a discussion of the sacred settings.

Before beginning a discourse on the musical virtues of the Whitman settings, it would be well to examine some of the reasons for Whitman's popularity among American composers in general and Dello Joio in particular. Some of the reasons advanced for Whitman's popularity among American composers are his frequent use of musical allusions and analogies, the oratorical gesture in his lines, his sense of emotional immediacy, and his emphasis upon the worth of the individual. For Dello Joio however, the most compelling reason is Whitman's "broad-scaled vision of an ideal world."[2] Whitman espoused the principles of democracy. For Whitman, American democracy was more than just a fervent parochial nationalism. It was a "spiritual democracy that encompasses all the peoples of the world."[3] Dello Joio's interest in this theme of spiritual democracy is evidenced not only by *Song of the Open Road, Take Our Hand Walt Whitman, Proud Music of the Storm,* and *Years of the Modern,* but also by his setting of lines from Stephen Vincent Benét's *Western Star* in the *Symphony for Voices and Orchestra* which predates all of the Whitman settings that relate to this theme. It is also likely that Dello Joio finds in Whitman a kindred spirit. Whitman classified music as a great moral force. He wrote in one of his editorials: "The subtlest spirit of a nation is expressed through its music—and music acts reciprocally upon the nation's very soul."[4] Whitman also advocated music for the masses stating: ". . . it must become more and more common, and more and more perfect, until the ability to sing well, and play some instrument, shall be as much a matter of course as the ability to read."[5] While Whitman's view of music as a moral force is probably more closely related to nineteenth century romantic ideals than contemporary thought, his advocacy of music for the masses would strike a sympathetic note with Dello Joio who has maintained a substantial interest in the field of music education in a democratic society, and has written several musical compositions that bring together masses of people, musicians and nonmusicians alike, for the purpose of sharing in the creation of a meaningful musical experience. Also significant is the fact that all of Dello Joio's Whitman settings are for chorus; none are for solo voice. He sees a "kind of transcendental element in his (Whitman's) writing," and feels that "the all embracing quality that it has calls for a choral setting."[6]

Dello Joio has taken an individual approach in setting Whitman to music.[7] Seven of his eleven settings are the sole example of that poem in the musical literature. He has been quite adventurous in his adaptation of Whitman for musical purposes. None of the poems are set to music exactly as Whitman wrote them, and the adaptation of the longer poems is quite extensive. He takes mere fragments from widely separated lines of the poem and arranges them to suit his own purposes. Dello Joio is forthright in stating that the words are not by, but are adapted from Whitman. However, even when making extensive alterations in the lines of poetry, the composer is always careful to preserve the spirit of the poem. He does not make revisions simply for the sake of accommodating a conventional musical structure, but is more interested in a direct, straightforward type of expression. Note Whitman's lines from "Proud Music of the Storm."

> Give me to hold all sounds, (I madly struggling cry.)
> Fill me with all the voices of the universe,

> Endow me with their throbbings, Nature's also,
> The tempests, waters, winds, operas and chants,
>   marches and dances,
> Utter, pour in, for I would take them all![8]

Dello Joio's version is:

> I struggling cry to hold all sounds,
> O to be filled with the voices of the universe,
> Nature, endow us with your throbbings,
> The tempests, the waters, the wind,
> God's chants and psalms, O! the marches, the dances,
> Utter! Pour in! I would take them all.

Dello Joio's first Whitman setting was completed during the early years of World War II. He selected from *Drum Taps* the poem "Vigil Strange," the text of which concerns a soldier who stands vigil over his fallen comrade. The poem explores a single human emotion—grief. The setting for mixed chorus and piano (four hands) is in a syllabic style with flowing, arched phrases for the choir. Text painting may be observed in the ascending melodic motion of the words "bathed in the rising sun," and the composer attempts to create a musical synonym by utilizing a humming chorus over the words "cool blew the night wind." Triads are mixed freely with seventh chords and quartal harmony (chords built on the interval of a fourth as opposed to triads which are built in thirds) to create a mildly dissonant to consonant sound consistent with the mood of the the text. The tonality is ambiguous as it moves freely among several key areas while a slow tempo and a steady quarter-note pulse maintain a contemplative mood throughout. It is a well conceived setting that is bound to make an impact on the sensitive listener.

Unlike *Vigil Strange* which has been set to music only once, *The Mystic Trumpeter* (1943) is but one of a dozen or so musical settings of this poem that date back to the turn of the century. "The theme of the poem is music's inspiration. The poet chose the trumpet perhaps because it was— in the conch stage—one of the most ancient and primitive of instruments. The general figure is the presence of music, inherent in nature, life, and the memory of things. The first five cantos invoke the memory of past musicians, especially those who bring back the romantic periods of history which embody the eternal dreams of lovers. But in canto 6 begins an antiphonal theme—the heralding of war . . . and finally comes the magnificent resolution of the concluding canto, wherein man is redeemed, society is utopian, and all is joy."⁹

Most composers have found the length and stanzaic structure of this poem to be ideal for a cantata with chorus, soloists, and orchestra. Dello Joio is the exception in that his setting calls for mixed chorus and solo French horn. In spite of the title, the choice is appropriate because the French horn probably approximates the sound of the ancient, primitive trumpet more closely than the modern trumpet. Dello Joio selected his text from cantos 1–3 and 5–8. Canto 4 is a curious omission as it evokes the pageantry of the feudal world with troubadours singing. The through-composed work divides into three sections with the text of canto 5 set as a slow, lyrical section for double chorus, soprano and tenor soloists. The outer sections feature fast tempos, martial rhythms, and frequent metric changes. The choral writing is declamatory with the use of choral speech called for in canto 7. The frequent use of fourths and fifths in parallel motion creates an archaic flavor as the poet calls forth the image of the ancient, "mystic trumpeter." Vocally the work is very demanding as it requires forceful climaxes and extended range (low C for the basses and high B for the sopranos). It was written for Robert Shaw and the Collegiate Chorale, and Dello Joio evidently had in mind the capabilities of that group when he wrote the work.

Commissioned by G. Schirmer for the High School of Music and Art in New York City, *A Jubilant Song* (1946) was adapted from Whitman's poem "A Song of Joys." It is another exuberant piece reflecting Whitman's call to delight and have faith in all things. The setting is for full chorus of mixed voices with piano (there is also a setting for female voices). The use of repeated motives in the accompaniment serves to generate energy and driving motion while the use of sharp dissonances of the major seventh variety creates bright colors which reflect the jubilant nature of the text. The use of E major, a bright key, also contributes to this effect. A ternary form is employed in which the third section is closely related to the first. Following the calm middle section, the exuberance of the opening section returns and culminates in a "La La La" refrain, the melody of which is a rhythmic augmentation of the sixteenth note motive from the accompaniment of section one.

The timing of these first three Whitman settings has a timely relationship to historical events. *Vigil Strange*, a profound expression of grief, was composed during the early years of World War II when the Allied forces were suffering one setback after another. *The Mystic Trumpeter*, which contrasts the hopes and dreams of lovers with the ravages of war, but in the end offers hope for the future, was written at a time when the tide of battle was turning in favor of the Allies. *A Jubilant Song* is an unrestrained expression of joy following the successful conclusion of the war.

Song of the Open Road (1952) was commissioned by the State University of New York for the Crane Department of Music, Potsdam State Teachers College. Dello Joio adapted his text from Whitman's poem of the same title, and subtitled the work "A Choral Proclamation." The setting is for mixed chorus, trumpet, and piano. With this work, the composer has taken thirty-four of the original two-hundred twenty-five lines and shaped them into a conventional three part form (ABA' and coda) that still express the basic Whitman ideology of the road as the symbol of an active and varied life in which man explores the unseen mysteries of the universe. It is interesting to note how Dello Joio's harmonic scheme relates to Whitman's call to adventure. The note F-sharp serves as the tonal center throughout most of the piece, with C-sharp functioning as its dominant. The A' section closes on a C-major chord (page 28, bar 3), but beginning on page 29, the coda seems to be headed back to F-sharp. That is not to be, however, as Dello Joio sidesteps to E and closes with a tremendous climax on the E-major triad. Life is an adventure; we are heading down new paths, not returning to the old ones from whence we came.

The musical content of *Song of the Open Road* is significant not only because of its relationship to the text, but also because it reveals a number of practices that have become more and more common in Dello Joio's choral writing. First is the use of tritonal relationships. The movement from the tonal area of F-sharp to that of C in the A' section of *Open Road* is a gradual one that takes place over some sixty measures. In later compositions these two harmonic areas are heard either in immediate succession or simultaneously as in the "Petrouchka chord" mentioned in Chapter 1. Second is the practice of starting a phrase with the voices in unison and expanding chromatically in both directions. This has the effect of first building tension and then releasing it as the harmonic intervals progress to minor second, major second, minor third, etc. This type of phrase can be observed in example 2.

Third is the use of the principle of organic growth. A small seed or thematic cell is planted in the piano introduction and the musical content grows and develops from this tiny cell. Dello Joio first used a thematic cell in some of his instrumental compositions such as *Concert Music* (1944), but this marks the first extensive use of this structural principle

Example 2. *Song of the Open Road,* page 15, bars 1–2

in a choral work. In *Song of the Open Road* the seed is planted with the minor third descent from A to F-sharp by the piano in bars 1 and 2. As the work progresses, the musical phrases are united by their common dependence on this interval. Note in example 3 how the declamatory phrases all either begin or end with a minor 3d.

Example 3. *Song of the Open Road,* bars 1–24

Beginning in bar 55 (example 4) the melodic writing becomes more expansive and lyrical, but the minor 3d is ever-present in each phrase. This is true of the entire score as the minor 3d is incorporated into motivic figures in the piano accompaniment as well as the melodic material assigned to the trumpet (see bars 23–24 and 76–80).

Example 4. *Song of the Open Road,* page 14, bars 1–2

Song of the Open Road may also serve to illustrate other aspects of Dello Joio's writing. An examination of example 3 will reveal his method of establishing tonality, his use of the introduction as an indicator of things to come, and the manner in which he uses the musical elements to achieve an effective climax to the musical phrase.

The tonality of F-sharp minor is established by reiteration at important structural points. The melodic descent from A to F-sharp in bars 1 and 2 combines with the fact that F-sharp functions as the root of the C-sharp–F-sharp dyad in bar 2 (Hindemith's method of calculating the harmonic value of intervals) to place the structural weight on F-sharp. The F-sharp11 chord in bar 7, the melodic ascent from C-sharp to F-sharp in bar 10, and the entrance by the basses and altos on F-sharp and A respectively all reinforce the note F-sharp as the tonal center. Beginning in bar 15 a series of nonfunctional chords culminates on the C-sharp major triad in bar 22 which functions as the dominant of the F-sharp9 chord which follows in bar 23. The C naturals in bars 1–4 not only function as chromatic neighbors to C-sharp but also assist in establishing the tritonal relationship with F-sharp that becomes important later in the composition. In this context the D9 chords in bars 6 and 8 are heard as tonic elaborations, and the B-minor chord in bar 10 takes on a subdominant function.

The first important climax in *Open Road* is heard in bar 20 as the choir sings the words, "Come travel with me" (Whitman's call to adventure). In achieving an effective climax, the composer may increase the level of tension in one or more musical elements by various means. Rising pitch level, increasing rhythmic and textural density, crescendo, and increasing degrees of dissonance are all effective means of building a climax. In this case the climax is achieved primarily by the rising melodic line from the basses F-sharp in bar 13 to the sopranos G-sharp in bar 20, and increasing textural density from one voice to five. Rhythmic density and level of dissonance remain fairly constant throughout the phrase. This pattern is repeated with ever-increasing intensity until the final E-major chord, which has all voices in their extreme upper register and added 2ds and 4ths in the keyboard for textural density and weight, is crowned by the trumpet's high B.

Following the composition of *Song of the Open Road* fourteen years elapsed before Dello Joio set Whitman to music again. Beginning in 1966, three major works were produced in consecutive years. *Songs of Walt Whitman* for chorus and orchestra (1966) received its first performance on 20 August 1966 at Interlochen, Michigan, during the International Society for Music Education (ISME) conference that was held there. The work was commissioned by the National Music Camp for the seventh biennial conference festival of ISME. *Proud Music of the Storm* for mixed chorus, brass, and organ (1967) was premiered on 27 November 1967. It was commissioned by Mr. and Mrs. Ralph J. Corbett for the one-hundredth anniversary celebration of the Cincinnati College Conservatory of Music. Commissioned by the Samuel S. Fels Fund for the twentieth anniversary of Singing City, the interracial choral complex at the Philadelphia Academy of Music, *Years of the Modern* for mixed chorus, brass, and percussion (1967–68) received its world premiere on 19 March 1968.

Songs of Walt Whitman consists of four movements of classical balance and proportion. The contrasting emotions of grief (movements 1 and 3) and joy (movements 2 and 4) are expressed in a style that reflects the compositional practices outlined in the discussion of *Song of the Open Road*. The musical content of each movement is derived from a brief thematic idea that is stated in the introduction. Although the individual movements are not united in a cyclical manner by the use of common themes, tritonal relationships provide a uniform color in the harmonic and melodic elements. In the dirgelike first movement, "I Sit and Look Out," the B-flat triad which serves as the tonal center is juxtaposed to the E triad at significant points in the instrumental interludes, and the tritone is heard often as a melodic or harmonic interval in the voice parts. The tritone is exploited even further in the second movement, "The Dalliance

of Eagles," as the entire instrumental introduction consists of the simultaneous presentation of major triads whose roots are a tritone apart. The
musical content of "Tears," the third movement, is summarized in the
intervalic relationships of the slowly arpeggiated opening chord which
contains two tritones (Db–G and A–Eb). Tritonal relationships are exploited to the ultimate degree in the final movement, "Take Our Hand
Walt Whitman," as they maintain the level of tension and excitement until
the final resolution on E major.

Text painting is used effectively in movement 3 as the words "stream-
ing tears" are set to streams of sixteenth notes in scalar movement (bar
55). The treatment of the text is also noteworthy in the fourth movement. Dello Joio adapted his text from "Salut au Monde!" Whitman's
lengthy poem is just what the title suggests, a salute to all the peoples
and places of the world which he portrays in long catalog descriptions.
Dello Joio has taken selected lines from the poem and reshaped them
into a work that calls upon all people to work together to build that utopian society of which Whitman speaks in several of his writings.

Whitman's catalogs have been the subject of much literary criticism.
For the uninitiated reader, a brief sample is quoted below.

> I hear the Arab muezzin calling from the top of the mosque,
> I hear the Christian priest at the altars of their churches,
>   I hear the responsive bass and soprano
> I hear the cry of the Cossack, and the sailor's voice
>   putting to sea at Okotsk,
> I hear the wheeze of the slave-coffle as the slaves
>   march on, as the husky gangs pass on by twos and
>   threes, fastened together with wrist-chains and
>   ankle-chains,
> I hear the Hebrew reading his records and psalms,
> I hear the rhythmic myths of the Greeks, and the
>   strong legends of the Romans,
> I hear the tale of divine life and bloody death of
>   the beautiful god the Christ. . . .[10]

Dello Joio's approach to the catalog was to try to capture some of the
cumulative dramatic force of Whitman's lines in musical terms. In *Take
Our Hand Walt Whitman* he accomplishes this by constructing a series
of "chain reaction phrases which rise to a climax."[11] The soprano line of
bars 47–58 is quoted in example 5 as an illustration. This dramatic treatment of the text is supported by the full orchestra and three additional

Example 5. *Take Our Hand Walt Whitman,* soprano line, bars 47–58

We hear the muez-zin from the   top of his mosque,   the

He - brew read-ing his scrolls and his   psalms,   the myths of Greeks, the

le - gends of Ro - mans ____   We hear   the   song   of the

Christ   child,   We hear the   songs sung by Ma - ry, His   moth - er,

brass choirs to bring the work to a rousing climax in the manner of a musical "Salut Au Monde."

Proud Music of the Storm and *Years of the Modern* are closely related to *Song of the Open Road.* The three poems have a common literary theme—a call to go forward hand in hand and face the future together. This is reinforced by a common musical theme that is derived from the tenor melody in bar 1 of example 4. In *Years of the Modern,* the descending 3d is contracted to a 2d (bar 136, bass line) and in *Proud Music* the ascending 5th is reduced to a 4th (bar 42, soprano line). These ideas are manipulated by inversion, augmentation, diminution, and other means of alteration as they serve as a unifying force in their respective compositions.

In addition to this common thematic bond, these three works have other features in common. All are composed in a single movement that divides into several contrasting sections. The fast sections emphasize energetic rhythmic patterns and declamatory writing while melodic lyricism is more characteristic in the slow sections. The tritone is very prominent, particularly in *Proud Music of the Storm,* as the organ introduction begins with trills on the notes E and B-flat and the voices enter later humming this same interval. Finally, in each of these works, Dello Joio was able to capture on his musical canvas Whitman's eternal optimism regarding the future and mankind's ultimate destiny. It is as though the composer was issuing a call to today's young people to move forward with Whitman and listen to the sounds of a new day.

Of the nineteen remaining secular choral works, three are substantial pieces for chorus and orchestra, one is for chorus and brass choir, and the rest are short pieces for chorus and piano.

The *Symphony for Voices and Orchestra* was commissioned by Robert Shaw who premiered it on 28 April 1945 with the Collegiate Chorale; Eileen Farrell, soprano; Robert Merrill, baritone; Joseph Laderoute, tenor; and Frederick Hart as narrator. Dello Joio culled his text from various passages in Stephen Vincent Benét's epic poem, "Western Star." The first movement, entitled "Virginia," deals with the desire of those in England destined to become the first pioneers from that country to America. The second movement, "New England," is a Pilgrim's prayer asking that God sustain them in their attempt to build a "New Zion." The last movement, "The Star in the West," has to do with the essential restlessness and progressiveness of Americans from the earliest colonial days to the present. According to the *New York Times* review, the work was brilliantly performed and well received by the capacity crowd. Dello Joio, however, felt that it had too many weaknesses and withdrew the score from circulation.

In 1953, when Dello Joio was commissioned by Cornell College in Iowa to compose a large work to be presented in the final festival concert of their centennial celebration, he took the score of *Symphony for Voices and Orchestra* and recast it into a symphonic cantata for chorus, narrator, soprano soloist, and full orchestra which he titled *Song of Affirmation*. This version of the work was premiered in May of that year with the Cornell Oratorio Society, Jennie Tourel as soloist, the composer as narrator, and members of the Chicago Symphony under the direction of Rafael Kubelik. The major revisions were made in movements 1 and 3. Movement 2 was left virtually intact. Basically the latter work is a condensation of the material from the former with some new sections added. The tenor and baritone solos were eliminated, and the material was shaped into a chain of motetlike musical statements of the text that move with cumulative dramatic force toward a climax. In the earlier version, ideas were treated symphonically by presentation and development to great length. The problem was that the music tended to get bogged down in the lengthy sections in which the composer tried to develop ideas that didn't lend themselves well to symphonic development.

To Saint Cecilia, a cantata for mixed chorus and brass ensemble, was commissioned by the University of Kansas, and premiered at the MENC national convention in Kansas City in 1959. The text was adapted from John Dryden's "A Song for St. Cecilia's Day," a poem intended, in Dello Joio's words, as a "big hymn glorifying music in the cosmic sense—the miracle of it all." Dello Joio's lyric gift is very evident in this through-composed work. The writing, in keeping with the "heavenly harmony" of the text, is almost entirely triadic, using seventh and ninth chords to build tension and resolving them to major triads. Strong dissonances are avoided. The beautifully shaped phrases and the logic of the voice leading would make the Renaissance masters sit up and take notice. The writing for brass often has the rich sonorities of a cathedral organ. This is one of the most stunningly beautiful scores to come from Dello Joio's pen.

Evocations for mixed chorus and orchestra was completed 16 July 1970 and given its premiere in October of that year at Tampa, Florida's first arts festival, "Generation 70." The work is cast in two movements of a contrasting nature. The first, "Vistants at Night," is based on Robert Hillyer's poem, "Visitants in a Country House at Night," which concerns an encounter with visitors from the "other world." In the poem, the visitors are a young man who lost his life on the hill at Verdun in World War I, and the young maid who took her own life to avenge the bullet that took the life of her lover. In Dello Joio's adaptation, the hill at Verdun becomes the hill at Saigon. He inserted his own statement, "Can Spring come again?" to relate to the second movement, "The Promise of Spring."

"Visitants at Night" is a very evocative piece in which the composer skillfully uses the musical resources to create a chilling atmosphere appropriate to the text. Dissonant chords, such as the whole tone clusters in measure 99, and short chromatic figures in the accompaniment contribute to that effect. Once again the three musical devices that were first noted in *Song of the Open Road* are present—tritonal relationships, the outward chromatic expansion from a close interval to larger intervals, and the use of a unifying motive (Bb Eb Db Bb) which is common to both movements.[12]

The second movement is based on the poem "Spring" by Richard Hovey. It is a joyful celebration of the coming of spring that calls for an additional young people's chorus to join the existing forces. Set in an ABA' form, the work features two ostinato patterns in the bass of the accompaniment, the second of which is used imitatively in the A' section as a "La La La" refrain for the choir. The unifying motive is first sung in an altered form by the sopranos in bar 22. It is announced by the trumpets in its original form at bar 42 and serves as the principal melodic idea in the polyphonic slow section for the chorus. In the final section it is stated boldly by the young people's chorus (bar 341) and the tenors and basses of the main choir (bar 345).

In spite of the unifying motive, the two movements of *Evocations* are not inseparable. "The Promise of Spring" is not difficult to perform and would make an effective climax at any music festival. Dello Joio rescored it for band and chorus for the dedication of the new Fine Arts Center at the University of Wisconsin-Eau Claire in 1971.

Among the shorter secular choral works there are lighthearted pieces such as *A Fable, Of Crows and Clusters,* and *Leisure,* as well as the more poignant settings which include *Madrigal, The Bluebird, Adieu, Mignonne, When You Are Gone, Songs End, The Poets Song,* and *Come to Me My Love.* Also of interest are *Three Songs of Chopin* arranged for both SA and SATB with piano or orchestra. The lighter pieces reveal a clever wit that is seldom to be found in the longer works, while the more serious pieces exhibit the composer's bent toward lyricism and effective part writing. All of these works are impressive utilitarian pieces that would be a worthy addition to the repertoire of any high school or college choir.

It is significant but not surprising that Dello Joio's most impressive sacred choral works were not written for the church, but for the concert hall. His experience as an organist/choir director during his youth made him aware of the meager musical resources of most churches, and discouraged him from writing church music, particularly during the early years of his career when he was trying to establish a reputation as a composer of serious music. It has only been during the later years of his career after his reputation was firmly established that he has written music for liturgical use.

Dello Joio's first composition to a sacred text was commissioned by the State University of New York for performance at the Potsdam Spring Festival in 1951. For this occasion he wrote *A Psalm of David,* an extended work for mixed chorus, strings, brass and percussion. It is thematically based on the plainchant "Miserere mei Deus" which Josquin Des Prez (1450–1521) used for an extensive setting of the same Psalm (no. 50 in the Catholic numbering, no 51 in the Protestant and Jewish numbering). Dello Joio borrowed his Latin text as well as the theme from Josquin. An English text from the King James version is also provided. The structure of the piece is explained by the composer in the preface to the score and need not be repeated here. The choral writing suggests early Renaissance church style by the frequency of open sounds—

fourths, fifths, and octaves, and by the emphasis on linearity in the individual voice parts. This results, particularly in part 1, in a rather bland harmonic style. The scoring is calculated for splendid, powerful sonorities.

O Sing unto The Lord, a setting of Psalm 98 for three part male chorus and organ, was commissioned by Yale University to commemorate the 200th anniversary of its chapel and was completed in 1958. The work exploits the tritonal relationship of C and F-sharp (G♭) with C ultimately establishing itself as the principal tonality. Structurally the work is through-composed with a new musical phrase for each line of text. Homophonic texture prevails in the voice parts while there is some use of counterpoint in the organ accompaniment. Frequent use of parallel chords and seventh chords is characteristic of the harmonic language.

For the Newman Choir of St. Cloud, Minnesota, Dello Joio composed *Prayers of Cardinal Newman* in 1960 to a text translated from the Roman Missal by John Henry Cardinal Newman (1801–90). This work consists of two short devotional pieces written in a very conservative style close to the common practice period.

For the occasion of the 125th anniversary of St. Mary's College, Notre Dame, Indiana, Dello Joio was commissioned to write a Mass utilizing the new English version of the Liturgy. The *Mass* was premiered on 7 December 1969, in the Church of Our Lady of Loretto on the campus of St. Mary's College. Using a voicing and instrumentation selected to fit the acoustics of the church, Dello Joio scored the work for mixed choir, brass choir, and organ. In the manner of the Renaissance Cantus Firmus Mass, the five movements of the Ordinary were composed based on a five note cell derived from the "Ite Missa Est" motive that Dello Joio had used earlier in *New York Profiles* (see chapter 3) and used later in *Psalm of Peace*. Except for the Sanctus, the different sections of the Mass are unified by virtue of the fact that all of the thematic material is based on this motive. As a whole the *Mass* is in a conservative style, rhythmically uncomplicated, never far from the consonant, and easily singable.

Dello Joio has written two other masses based on the English liturgy— *Mass in Honor of the Blessed Virgin Mary* and *Mass in Honor of the Eucharist*. Both were written in 1975, both omit the Credo, and both are written in a simple manner with much unison singing.

The final sacred work to be considered is the *Psalm of Peace* for mixed chorus, trumpet, French horn, and organ. Composed in 1972, the work was commissioned by the Oratorio Society of Montgomery County, Bethesda, Maryland, for its tenth anniversary season. Like *Psalm of David*,

Example 6. "Ite Missa Est" motive used in *Psalm of Peace*

this work is also based on a plainchant and divides into three sections. The chant is the "Ite Missa Est" motive stated in example 6.[13]

Following his tendency to compose from a small seed, Dello Joio derives not only the musical content, but also the formal structure from the notes of this motive. The motetlike chain of statements are built on the stepwise entrances of variant *a* in parts 1 and 2 covering the ascending range of a 7th from D to C-sharp. Note that the chant also covers the range of a 7th. Part 3 is based on the stepwise entrances of variant *b* covering the descending range of a 5th from E to A, the 5th being the largest interval encountered in the chant melody. By means of thematic transformation Dello Joio was able to give each section of the Psalm its own character according to the demands of the text, and unify the whole with a common thematic bond.

Example 7. *Psalm of Peace,* thematic variants

Dello Joio has not been as prolific in writing for the solo voice as he has been in writing for the choral ensemble. Nevertheless, his solo vocal works represent a significant contribution to the solo vocal literature of the past four decades and merit discussion at this point.[14]

His earliest songs date from the years 1937–39, when he was a student at the Institute of Musical Art. The first is a spirited piece titled "Ballad of Thomas Jefferson," with words by Louis Lerman. It is written in a somewhat popular style that pays homage to the folk ballads of the colonial period. Three other songs date from this period, all of them settings of poems by Carl Sandburg (1878–1967). "Gone" is for high voice and piano while "Joy" and "Mill Doors" are both for baritone and piano.[15] Of the three, "Mill Doors" is the only one that has been published. Although composed during Dello Joio's student years, it is a finely hewn work that reveals the kind of craftsmanship found in his more mature works. Dello Joio uses a binary song form that corresponds to the two strophes of Sandburg's poem dealing with the exploitation of the American working man by industrialized society. A slowly moving melody in the phrygian mode is accompanied by dissonant chords that serve to express the anguish felt by the etcher of this brief poem. Descriptive effects, such as the use of a rhythmic ostinato to express monotony, and open fifths and octaves to express a feeling of emptiness, also play a key role in making this song an effective fusion of music and poetry.

"New Born" and "There Is a Lady Sweet and Kind," both for medium voice and piano, date from the year 1946. With "New Born" Dello Joio used a poem by Lenore G. Marshall (1899–) as a pretext for writing a brief lullaby. The melody is written in the key of F major, and strong dissonances are avoided in order to be consistent with the soothing effect of the poem. Of greater musical and textual interest is the setting of the anonymous Elizabethan poem, "There Is a Lady Sweet and Kind." It is also written in the key of F major with a restrained use of dissonance, but a more varied harmonic scheme, more extensive melodic range, and the attractive piano interludes featuring running parallel thirds, make this a much more appealing song.

In 1947 Dello Joio composed two songs based on tragic themes—an execution and an assassination. "Lament" is a setting of the poem, "Elegy" which was written by the English writer Chidiock Tichborne (ca. 1558–1586) on the eve of his execution.[16] To capture the sense of tragedy and hopelessness expressed by the writer of this poem, Dello Joio used some of the same techniques that were successful in "Mill Doors." In the accompaniment to both songs, the ominous repetition of a single note, combined with a descending second figure, serves to create a sense of impending doom. In "Mill Doors" the use of the phrygian mode created a somber atmosphere. The minor mode serves the same purpose in "Lament." In both songs the composer uses the upper range of the voice at a forte dynamic level supported by strongly dissonant chords to express the anguish felt by the speaker in the poem. The structural relationship between the music and the poetry is also similar in the two songs. The two strophes of "Mill Doors" were set in binary (AB) form, whereas the three strophes of "Elegy" resulted in a ternary (ABA') form.

Although the tragic themes of "Mill Doors" and "Elegy" inspired similar musical treatment on the part of Dello Joio, his setting of "The Assassination" by Robert Hillyer is another matter. This song reveals a composer with a keen sense of dramatic effect and vocal characterization. Hillyer has sketched a dramatic dialogue between two "Fates" which, in

a personified state, conspire to kill "Hope." Dello Joio made an adaptation
of the poem that eliminates all of the narrative passages and retains only
the essential dialogue. He was then able to mold a through-composed
song in the form of a minidrama that moves swiftly to a climax. The music
functions operatically: it surrounds the drama with an atmosphere appropriate to the dramatic situation; it comments on the action; it supplies
inarticulate thoughts; and it characterizes for better or for worse the
characters in the drama. The murder, for example, takes place off stage.
We are dependent on the piano accompaniment to tell us what is happening at this point in the drama. Widely spaced dissonant chords exploit the
extreme ranges of the keyboard and the sustaining pedal is used to max-
imize the accumulation of dissonance in order to heighten the tension to
an appropriate level. Following this, the text "He's dead," is sung medium
range on a single pitch and marked "senza expressione" (without expression) in order to project the lack of emotion and detachment on the part
of the cold-blooded assassin. At other points character delineation is accomplished by melodic inflection, skillful rhythmic notation in the voice
line, and subtle changes in tempo. This instinct for effective dramatic
representation through music was later put to effective use in Dello Joio's
operas.

Turning away from the tragic themes of "Lament" and "The Assassination" Dello Joio next devoted his attention to the composition of a group
of love songs. Selecting English poets of the Victorian era and the Res-
toration period, he composed "Eyebright," "Why So Pale and Wan, Fond
Lover?" "Meeting at Night," "All Things Leave Me," and "How Do I
Love Thee?," all in 1948. In 1950 he chose a poem by the American
writer Stark Young (1881–1963) as the text of "The Dying Nightingale."
These songs were grouped together under the collective title of *Six Love
Songs*. However, they do not constitute a song cycle in the truest sense
of the term. To program any one of them on a recital would be
appropriate.

Each of the poems presents a different aspect of the abstract idea of
love. "Eyebright" by John Addington Symonds (1840–93) is an autobio-
graphical poem in which the poet pays tribute to a young woman whose
love proved to be a cure for his state of depression brought on by long
years of illness. Taken from the play *Aglaura* by Sir John Suckling (1609–
42), "Why So Pale and Wan Fond Lover?" cautions that love can lead to
frustration should the woman prove unwilling. In Robert Browning's
(1812–89) poem, "Meeting at Night," the brief but meaningful experience
found in a passionate encounter proves to be worth the struggle to

achieve it. In the case of "The Dying Nightingale" an idealistic view of love results in the ultimate sacrifice. The poem "Memory" by Arthur Symons (1865–1945) served as the text of "All Things Leave Me." It demonstrates the ability of love to completely capture the imagination and hold one spellbound. In the poem "How Do I Love Thee?" by Elizabeth Barret Browning (1806–61), love results in the complete dedication of one individual to another, both in life and in death.

The musical settings of *Six Love Songs* reveal Dello Joio's sensitivity to the language of the poet. There is evidence that such poetic devices as formal structure, meter, rhyme scheme, stress patterns, units of thought, and word meaning influenced the composer's choice of musical devices. In the case of "All Things Leave Me" the musical form is related to the rhyme scheme. The rhyming of stanzas 1 and 3 is paralleled by an ABA' song form. On the other hand, "Why So Pale and Wan Fond Lover?" is a three-stanza poem in which the third stanza is contrasted to the first by a change of accentual pattern and by a change from the interrogative to the imperative mood. This is paralleled by a musical form of AA'B. The subject of the poem "Meeting at Night" progresses toward his goal without hesitating or turning back. This fact is reflected in the music by the use of a through-composed form.

"Meeting at Night" is also noteworthy for the composer's use of various musical devices to suggest the sound, movement, and other effects implied by certain words in the text. The broad expanse of the beach and open fields is suggested by the wide spacing of the notes in the piano introduction and the comparatively long note values in the voice line. At the same time the use of dissonant seconds and sevenths and chromatic movement of the inner voices of the accompaniment provide the element of tension present in the subject who is anxious to reach his destination. The use of short note values and the upward skip of a third suggest both the size and movement of the waves under the text, "startled little waves that leap." In measures 32–37, heavy accents in the accompaniment combine with the octave leap upward in the voice to evoke a feeling of muscular strength involved in pushing the boat ashore. The use of a broken eighth note figure in measure 41 describes very well the breathless haste as the subject moves across the beach and fields to the farmhouse. The right hand figure in the accompaniment in measure 48 is a musical "tap at the pane." The convergence of two chromatic lines in the inner voices of the accompaniment bring the two people together, and the heavily accented quarter notes in measure 63 suggest the "two hearts beating each to each."

The other songs in this group also reveal a close correlation between music and text. Because of this and the variety of poets and poetic styles present, they make an interesting study in contrasts when performed as a group. Because three of the songs are for medium voice and three are for high voice, however, it would take a singer of exceptional range and dynamic control to present all of them on a recital.

"The Listeners" (1954) and "Un Sonetto di Petracara" (1959) provide a study in contrasts that further illustrates the expressive range of the composer. Based on a ghostly narrative by Walter De La Mare (1873–1956), "The Listeners" is written in a declamatory style in which the rapid repetition of single pitches combines with sharp registral contrasts, and persistent dissonance in the accompaniment to create the effect, the thrill, and the overtones of the haunted mansion in which the scene takes place. The setting of Francesco Petrarca's (1303–74) sonnet "Benedetta Sia'l Giorno," is a study in lyricism. Employing the original Italian, Dello Joio wrote a flowing melody which features shifting modality and at times neumatic or even melismatic treatment of the text, one of the rare occasions in which the composer departs from syllabic treatment in any of his vocal works. This type of melody is combined with a colorfully ornamented keyboard accompaniment to create an effective musical expression of Petrarca's salutation to his beloved Laura.

In 1960 Dello Joio composed two songs that celebrate the birth of the Christ child. The first is a setting of "A Christmas Carol" by G. K. Chesterton (1874–1936). "A Holy Infant's Lullaby," with a text by the composer, is taken from the score of *A Saintmaker's Christmas Eve* which he wrote for ABC-TV. The music of both of these songs is characterized by tenderness and simplicity. They are composed in a major key, utilize compound meter, and are in strophic form with symmetrical phrase structure.

In 1962 Dello Joio took the children's chorus from the last act of *Blood Moon*, arranged it for solo voice and piano, and published it under the title "Bright Star."[17] The music of this song is slightly more adventurous with its use of shifting modality and mixture of tertian and quartal harmony emphasizing parallel chords.

Three Songs of Adieu were composed in 1963. Unlike *Six Love Songs*, this set can rightly be considered a song cycle. The three songs are related textually by their common subject matter and musically by the use of a unifying melodic motive. Dello Joio selected the poems "After Love" by Arthur Symons and "Farewell" by John Addington Symonds as the texts of the first and third songs respectively. The author of "Fade

Vision Bright," the second song, is unknown. The collective theme of the three poems is that parting brings sorrow.

Musically, *Three Songs of Adieu* are outstanding for several reasons. In terms of melodic complexity and extreme range, they are among the most difficult songs the composer has written. Angular leaps are encountered in a melodic style that is close to becoming atonal. The harmony is based on the use of structural dissonance that is varied by degree to provide harmonic direction. In terms of compositional craft this cycle reveals an extremely close-knit structure based on the exploitation of a limited number of musical ideas.

Considering the complexity and difficulty of *Three Songs of Adieu*, one might ask why such an abrupt turnabout from the simplicity of the three Christmas songs. The answer lies in the composer's sensitivity to his subject matter. The complex, heartfelt emotions dealt with in *Three Songs of Adieu* call forth a cry of anguish, a primal scream if you will, to cope with frustration. Consequently the composer makes use of the extreme upper register of the singing voice accompanied by grinding dissonance on the keyboard to arouse a similar response from the listener. Another factor to be considered is that this cycle was written with Mary Costa's voice in mind. She had sung the lead soprano role in *Blood Moon* two years earlier, and Dello Joio was well acquainted with her capabilities.

"Note left on a Doorstep" was composed in 1969 as a gesture of appreciation to its author, Lily Peter, who had commissioned Dello Joio's *Homage to Haydn* for the celebration of the Arkansas sesquicentennial. The poem is a brief lyric about death that expresses the belief that death has power over the body, but not the spirit. To capture the serenity of expression found in this poem, Dello Joio composed a flowing, lyrical melody over mildly dissonant chords. B-flat serves as a tonal center while chromatic alterations are made freely. The accompaniment is bound together by the repetition of a single rhythmic pattern and a melodic sequence. Written in a through-composed form, the music is matched well to the sentiments expressed in the text.

Two works remain to be discussed in this chapter. The first is *The Lamentation of Saul*, a dramatic cantata that was composed between 20 June and 31 July 1954, for baritone solo, and chamber ensemble consisting of flute, oboe, clarinet, viola, cello, and piano. Commissioned by the Coolidge Foundation, the work received its premiere on 21 August 1954 in Pittsfield, Massachusetts, with a group of Boston Symphony musicians, the composer at the piano, and Leonard Warren as baritone soloist. In the fall of 1954 Dello Joio rescored the work for full orchestra for a performance by the Baltimore Symphony. The second is *Songs of Remembrance* for baritone solo and orchestra. This work was premiered on 26 August 1977 at the Saratoga Performing Arts Center with Eugene Ormandy conducting the Philadelphia Orchestra and baritone Alan Wagner. It was the second in a series of five Bicentennial commissions undertaken by the Saratoga Performing Arts Center from 1976 through 1980.

For *The Lamentation of Saul* Dello Joio adapted his text from the play *David* by D. H. Lawrence (1885–1930). Written in 1926, the play is based on the Biblical account of Saul's decline from God's favor and David's annointment as the next King of Israel as recorded in I Samuel, chapters 15–30 of the King James version. The work is composed in a single movement that divides into four sections with a tempo pattern of fast-slow-fast-slow. Dramatically, each section has a single purpose. Section 1 identifies Saul and his mission. Section 2 reveals his sin—defiance of God's commandment. A brief recitative that follows foretells the impending doom that awaits Saul as a result of his sin. Saul's realization of his sin is the message of section 3. In section 4 he laments and prays for reinstatement and forgiveness.

The vocal line in *Lamentation of Saul* is largely declamation, and the musical texture is written in a series of contrasting patterns intended to emphasize the message of the text. Larger units of meaning are defined by contrasts in meter, tempo, rhythmic and melodic patterns, and texture. Subsections are delineated by musical phrasing, type of melodic motion, harmonic area, textural and rhythmic contrasts. The tritonal relationship between F-sharp and C plays a significant role in this work just as it does in many of the choral works. It is sounded in a prophetic manner in the opening chord, and is used often as a melodic interval. In addition, the harmonic relationship of the F-sharp and C-major triads is used to create tension at most of the major climaxes. Although built around a tonal center of C, the work is characterized by frequent changes of mode. The use of the medieval modes underlines the Near East, Biblical nature of the text. The rhythmic element also contributes to the desired emotional impact. For example, section 1 features fast tempo, changing meter, shifting and conflicting accents, and changing patterns as its purpose is to identify Saul, the man of action.

It should be mentioned that when Dello Joio rescored the cantata for full orchestra, he composed an additional sixty-five bars of music. Most of this can be accounted for in the instrumental introduction which is lengthened from forty to eighty-five bars, and features a melody on the English horn not found in the original score. The other additional bars are scattered throughout the score as one or two bar extensions of instrumental interludes. Because of the increased variety of color and sheer fullness of sound, the orchestral version is probably more exciting. However, as a piece of chamber music, the original score can stand fully on its own merits by the effective use of the musical elements on a small scale.

The cycle *Songs of Remembrance* comprises settings of four poems by John Hall Wheelock—"The Revenant," "The Lion House," "Storm and Sun," and "Farewell to the House in Bonac"—which Dello Joio described as follows on the occasion of their first performance.

The first is an Andante moderato, a waltz. It is a song of a once remembered youthful love that has matured into a deeper feeling that comes with old age.

The second is a dramatic scene. It is a witnessing of a lion in its "bright prison of steel" pacing endlessly. The poet asks, "For the delight of whom?"

The third song, "Storm and Sun," is one of two lovers plunging into a stormy sea: heartfree, they share an exultation in meeting the fury of the deeps by leaving behind the little frets and fevers of everyday life. The poet concludes, "The might of moving waters around us is music! And on our faces the glory of God is shed."

The final song is a farewell to youth, to friends long gone, the house of memories the poet calls "the cradle and grave of my poems."

These poems are in settings as familiar to me as to Mr. Wheelock, since we both have homes on the sea at the far end of Long Island, New York, and I share deeply with him a love of a still unspoiled part of our land.[18]

"The Lion House" and "Storm and Sun" are powerful dramatic pieces that utilize the full resources of the modern orchestra. The prominence of low pitched instruments (bassoon and contra-bassoon, bass clarinet, English horn, trombone, tuba, cellos, and basses) serves to evoke the powerful image of the pacing lion in the former, while the orchestra is used to call forth the surging power and broad expanse of the sea in the latter. These two songs are flanked by the tender, lyrical settings of "The Revenent" and "Farewell to the House at Bonac," both of which are lightly scored for woodwinds, harp, and strings.

"The Lion House" is noteworthy because it is one of the very few examples of twelve-tone writing in Dello Joio's music. The first twenty-one bars are quoted in example 8 to illustrate his use of the technique. The song opens with the twelve tone row stated in octaves by the cellos

and basses. Beginning in bar 9, the oboe, English horn, clarinet, and
bassoon play a descending chromatic scale motive in counterpoint to the
repetition of the row. At bar 17, the voice enters singing the third statement of the row in its original form while the cellos and basses play it in
retrograde, and the woodwinds play an inverted augmentation of their
motive from bar 9. The four stanzas of the poem are set in ABA′ form
with stanzas 2 and 3 combining to form the middle section. The row and
its derivatives are abandoned in the B section, but return in the final
section. The row is stated in its entirety seven times, five times in A,
and twice in A′. Although it is based on a twelve-tone row, this song
remains strictly within the bounds of tonality with E-flat serving as the
tonal center. Note that the row itself begins on B-flat and ends on E-flat
thereby establishing a dominant-tonic relationship at the outset. The final
cadence is to an E-flat minor chord. Even though Dello Joio has shunned
the twelve-tone method in the vast majority of his compositions, this
song serves as evidence that he can use the principles of twelve-tone
writing to good effect when he chooses to do so.

Example 8. *The Lion House,* bars 1–21

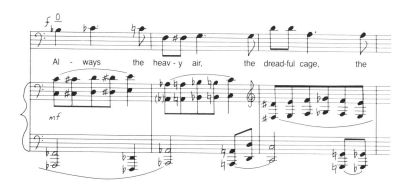

Al - ways the heav - y air, the dread-ful cage, the

Before concluding, it must be stated that Dello Joio's expectations of the baritone voice in this cycle are equally as demanding as those of his idol, Verdi. The tessitura lies high, and the baritone must possess the skill to deliver his top G with dramatic power on the final note of "Storm and Sun," and with a controlled pianissimo in the penultimate phrase of "Farewell to the House in Bonac."

The skillful construction and expressive power of *Songs of Remembrance* demonstrates that Dello Joio's creative powers are certainly not waning. Contemporary singers and their audience will be the beneficiaries should he continue to devote his energy to this area of composition that was comparatively neglected during the earlier years of his career.

3

Orchestral Works

Dello Joio's earliest compositions for orchestra date from his years as a graduate student at Juilliard. The first, composed in 1940, is a four movement work cast in a neoclassical symphonic mold entitled *Sinfonietta*. It was premiered 10 May 1941 at Juilliard. The orchestral score was published by G. Schirmer, but an unpublished two-piano version was used by Eugene Loring's Dance Players for the ballet *Prairie*, which premiered on 21 April 1942 in New York City. The writing shows certain characteristics that mark *Sinfonietta* as an early Dello Joio composition— a multiplicity of themes, and melodic construction that contains note patterns from several different keys—while at the same time revealing practices that would be retained in later compositions—sectional forms based on the principle of statement-departure-return, and a harmonic language consisting of extended tertian and quartal chords.

The second orchestral work composed during his student years was the *Magnificat* for chamber orchestra, which was composed between 7 July and 27 August 1942 in New Hope, Pennsylvania, the summer home of Loring's Dance Players for whom Dello Joio was serving as musical director at the time. This work came about as the result of a competition for a work for chamber orchestra sponsored by the Town Hall Music Committee. On the invitation of the committee, three institutions chose one of their respective composition students as entrants in the competition. The three students selected were Dello Joio of the Juilliard Graduate School, William Bergsma of the Eastman School of Music, and Allen Sapp of the Music Department of Harvard College. They were commissioned in June of 1942, and their works were premiered on 31 March 1943 by the Saidenberg Little Symphony under the direction of Daniel

Daniel Saidenberg. Dello Joio's efforts earned him the Town Hall Composition Award of 1943, which carried a prize of $250.00.

Magnificat marks a significant turning point in Dello Joio's career. In his own mind it represents a moving out of his student days into maturity as a composer. Having been composed so soon after he completed his studies with Hindemith, the work naturally shows the influence of the older master. Concerning this influence, Edward Downes wrote:

> Its importance to him lies in the clarification and ordering of his musical style he associated with Hindemith. More than once he recalls the Hindemith of *Mathis der Maler*, although *Magnificat* is not an imitative work. The influence shows first of all in the sturdy craftsmanship and a certain four square seriousness, which is by no means incompatible with an infectious exuberance in the livelier pages. It shows in the texture of the strongly contrapuntal writing, the frequent use of a cantus firmus technique of allotting the principle theme to the trumpet, horns or woodwinds, in unison or octaves, against a lively figuration in the strings and other instruments. It shows in the frequent organ-like registration of the orchestral sonorities. It shows in the careful use of (chiefly diatonic) dissonance. It shows in cadential progressions and in the archaic effects of fourths, fifths, and octaves with added seconds.[1]

Composed in a single movement and scored for piccolo, two flutes, two clarinets, trumpet, four horns, piano, percussion, and strings, *Magnificat* is modeled on the Vesper Canticle and inspired freely by Gregorian Chant. Structurally it resembles the classical rondo-sonata. The formal scheme of ABA'CA" is delineated by change of tempo as well as thematic idea. The energetic A section presents two contrasting ideas, one short and motivic, and the other an extended cantabile melody, that are developed in A' and recapitulated in A". Sections B and C provide slow, lyrical interludes. The influence of Gregorian Chant can be heard clearly in the opening section as the smoothly contoured lines are frequently doubled at the fourth or fifth.

In terms of the skillful construction, logical connection of ideas, and colorful instrumentation, *Magnificat* represents a significant step forward for the composer. Melodically, however, it is still more closely related to *Sinfonietta* than to his later works in this genre. The later works contain more compact melodic ideas and reveal Dello Joio's ability, not yet evident in these early works, to comprehend and exploit all of the inherent possibilities of his thematic ideas.

Dello Joio's next two works for orchestra were also written in a single movement with contrasting sections. *To a Lone Sentry* (composed 19–30 August 1943 while Dello Joio was in residence at the MacDowell Colony) was commissioned by the League of Composers, which at the time was commissioning various composers to write works for orchestra that related to the war.[2] It was premiered by the Baltimore Symphony in 1944. Dello Joio dedicated his work to the lonely sentries stationed over the world in a time of war. His intent was to portray the thoughts of such men—the nostalgic recollections of happier days which sustain men through such watches. The score begins with three bell-like tones from the celeste and an echoing trumpet played softly from behind the scenes to lend the effect of distance. This leads to a quiet, contemplative section for divisi strings and clarinet that grows gradually in interval stress until it breaks into a fast, energetic section that represents the happier, carefree days that occupy the thoughts of the sentry. It eventually sinks again to a contemplative ending with the echoing trumpet sounding in the distance.

Concert Music for orchestra was written during the summer of 1944, while Dello Joio was in residence at an artist colony in Silvermine, Connecticut. The work was first performed at Juilliard in 1945. The official world premiere took place on 4 January 1946, however, with Fritz Reiner conducting the Pittsburgh Symphony. For the program book, Dello Joio wrote the following description of its content:

In its general outline, it is a three part form. A main germinal rhythmic motive is immediately introduced by the tympani. This motive serves as a binding force throughout the composition. It is elaborated in an extended prologue which is followed by a first theme allegro, played by the high woodwinds against a rhythmic background of strings, brass, and tympani. A short development of this idea introduces elements which serve as a background to the second theme, songlike in character. A continual dovetailing of many variants of this theme takes place in various registers of the orchestra. This is followed by a return to the first theme presented in a new guise. This section is then brought to a high pitch of intensity, and eventually subsides to a formal pianissimo close.

Now the introduction re-appears in a new form in which it serves as a setting for the second section, andante. The long melodic line is played by violins and taken up by the flutes and oboes. An intensification is then supplied by the brass in the reiteration of the main melody. This part again closes softly and a gradual transition brings the piece back to the earlier rhythmic and restless character. The final section presents all of the previous themes and motives in a new form and order, continually juxtaposed against one another. This cumulative process brings the work to a triple forte ending.[3]

Dello Joio's description of "a main germinal rhythmic motive" fails to convey the melodic signifiance of this motive (example 9). Its intervallic structure is at least as important as its rhythmic structure in providing a "binding force throughout the composition." There are instances in which the rhythm of the motive is simply augmented, thus retaining the relative durational values (bar 255, trombones). Just as frequent, however, are passages in which the rhythmic structure is altered beyond recognition, but the pitch relationships are left intact (bars 54–60, low strings, woodwinds, and brass).

Example 9. *Concert Music,* bars 1–3

As important a role as the germinal motive plays in *Concert Music,* even more important are the implications for future works. As Dello Joio's style developed from the late forties onward, two important structural types emerged as the basic means of organization in his compositions—the variations form and the principle of organic growth based on a germinal motive or thematic cell.

The first of these to emerge was the variations form which Dello Joio first explored in the Concerto for harp and orchestra in 1945 (see chapter 6). It was in *Variations, Chaconne, and Finale,* however, that he first demonstrated mastery of the variation techinque. He began work on this composition in the spring of 1947, and completed it during the summer of that year while he was residing at his summer residence in Wilton, Connecticut.[4] The basic idea of the work had begun to formulate in his mind much earlier. For a performance of the work in Cincinnati in 1949, he wrote:

The work of mine that Cincinnati is to hear is the result of a fixation. I held my first professional position as organist at twelve years of age, and it was sometime in that dim past that I first heard and played the theme of *Variations* in its original Gregorian form. [See example 10.] For years I improvised and mulled it over in my mind. Last year I finally got down to doing what I thought a valid exposition of a simple idea.[5] At present I am engrossed in the variation form for I find it a most satisfying medium for the investigation of the potentials of a theme.[6]

Once again the world premiere took place in Pittsburgh with Reiner conducting.[7] After its Pittsburgh premiere on 30 January 1948 *Variations* enjoyed many performances under the baton of Franco Autori who toured Poland with the work in 1948. Bruno Walter conducted the New York premiere on 9 December 1948 and Thor Johnson introduced it in Boston on 21 January 1949.

Example 10. "Kyrie" from the *Mass of Angels,* which Dello Joio used as the theme of *Variations, Chaconne, and Finale*

Ky - ri -   e   -   -   -   -   -   e   -   -   le - i - son

The Gregorian theme (example 10) is the subject for a set of variations in the first movement and is introduced in different form in the second and third movements. The first movement consists of a simple harmonized statement of the theme followed by six variations. At the opening, the five bar theme is stated three times—first by the solo oboe, then by clarinet and flute with string harmonization, and finally in an extended phrase in which fragments of the theme are passed among woodwinds and strings. The harmonization is mild as the individual lines progress smoothly through a succession of seventh and ninth chords. The G-major orientation is infused with non-functional progressions. The syncopated cadence leading to a tonic ninth chord creates a somewhat unfinished effect that is finally alleviated in the coda following variation 6 as the pizzicato strings sound a unison G.

Variation 1 (semplice e grazioso, $\downarrow$. = 56) continues the simple, graceful character of the theme. A variant derived from the first twelve notes of the theme is heard in a lilting 6/8 rhythm against an accompanying pattern that emphasizes parallel thirds against a repeated pitch. In the middle section the G-major orientation shifts to E-flat.

Variation 2 (andante religioso, $\downarrow$ = 60) is even more contemplative. Scored for nine-part divisi strings and woodwinds, it moves through a rich progression of block chords with the theme concentrated in the first violins.

Variation 3 (vivacissimo, $\downarrow$ = 176) provides the first departure from the basic religious nature of the theme. In a rapid 3/4 meter, the melody undergoes abbreviation, fragmentation, octave displacement, and other permutations. Brass and percussion are heard for the first time in this movement.

Variation 4 (allegro pesante, $\downarrow$ = 76) continues the animated character of the previous variation. It is a fast section of propulsive energy.

Beginning in bar 145, two voices in quasicanonical relation follow one another in restless succession. The voices are formed by short, mainly scalewise motives that are derived from the first two bars of the theme. Irregular cross accents and frequent rests between the motivic fragments result in a disjointed, agitated feeling.

Variation 5 (amabile, ♩ = 56) resembles variation 1 in style, form, mood, and tonality. The lilting 6/8 rhythm returns and the accompaniment now consists of parallel sixths under a repeated tonic. The melody, which is played chiefly by bassoon and cello, is clearly derived from the first two bars of the theme.

Variation 6 (funebre, ♩ = 52) is the least obvious in terms of its relation to the theme. Set in a slow, evenly paced manner, the melody sounds in the upper register of the woodwinds against slowly undulating harmonies by strings and brass. The rather tenuous relation to the theme combines with remote tonal regions to create an aura of suspense about this variation. This is quickly dispelled, however, with the return to G major in the brief coda that follows.

Dello Joio stated that the "framework on which the *Chaconne* is built is a chromatic outline of the first four notes of the theme."[8] Here he adopted a plan similar to that used by Brahms for the fourth movement of his fourth symphony—a set of variations built over a rising chromatic line that is repeated every eight bars. The movement, which consists of sixteen variations and coda, builds with cumulative dramatic force toward one tremendous climax in variation thirteen (bars 92–108), and then tapers off into the coda, which is a synthesis of everything that came before. Building on the gradual increase in tension implied by the chromatic theme, Dello Joio uses the elements of rhythm, harmony, and texture to mount his climax. The gradual addition of instruments combines with an increase in rhythmic activity and intervallic stress to achieve the desired goal.

In the final movement, an Allegro vivo, the character of the Gregorian theme is transformed into the purely secular as dance rhythms abound. In the concluding pages the theme is presented by the brass in the form of a chorale against the prevailing rhythmic tension of the other instruments. It is this final movement that probably inspired the original title of the work—*Three Symphonic Dances.*

Following closely on the heels of *Variation, Chaconne, and Finale* were *Serenade for Orchestra* (1948) and *New York Profiles* (1949). *Serenade* is the concert title of a dance score written for Martha Graham. She premiered the work in the summer of 1948 under the title *Wilderness*

Stair. The title was later changed to *Diversion of Angels*, and that work became a staple in the repertoire of her company. The score was composed as an abstract piece, not set to any particular dance thought, but according to Dello Joio, it embodied the exalted and extroverted movement in which Miss Graham was interested. For the orchestral premiere on 20 October 1949 by George Szell and the Cleveland Orchestra, Dello Joio enlarged the scoring but made no other changes in the original score. He described the work as "a dedication to the outdoors," and said about it, "I use throughout a constant juxtaposition of two distinct qualities— lyrical and athletic.[9] These two elements I have fused into a tonal picture of my conception of, or reaction to, the out-of-doors."[10]

Serenade is cast in the form of a free rondo. An introduction suggests the athletic character of the swift sections that are to follow. Then the lyrical theme is introduced in an imitative contrapuntal texture beginning with the flute and followed by the other woodwinds. This section is extended by the use of thematically derived motives until a cadence on a B-minor ninth chord, from which is derived the underlying ostinato pattern of the con anima e spumante (with animation and sparkle) section which follows. The theme of this section is introduced by the first violins at bar 93, and this proves to be the main part of the rondo. It returns with varied treatment following three intervening lyrical episodes each with its own theme. The final section offers a brilliant climax with the piccolo predominant in reiterations of the two principal subjects.

New York Profiles for chamber orchestra was commissioned by Augustus L. Searle for the Musical Arts Society of La Jolla, California. The world premiere took place on 21 August 1949 with Nicolai Sokoloff conducting. Here Dello Joio has painted a series of musical pictures depicting notable landmarks in his native city. Movement 1, "The Cloisters," employs once again the Gregorian chant "Ite Missa Est" (example 6) to evoke images of the monastery overlooking the Hudson river. The modal-based linear writing is highly effective and only incidentally archaic. Movement 2, "The Park," is a frolicking caprice depicting children at play. Rhythmic ostinati maintain a high level of energy throughout as fragments of children's songs are bandied about in the orchestral texture, slightly varied each time they return. Movement 3, "The Tomb," refers to Grant's tomb. It is in the form of a chorale fantasy with occasional motives from the "Ite Missa Est" chant providing a thematic bond to the first movement. It depicts the tragedy rather than the glory of war as the modal melodies and chord progressions produce a somber atmosphere—a hint at the terrible misfortunes of a long ago conflict that must

not be forgotten. The "Ite Missa Est" theme also plays a significant role in the last movement, "Little Italy." In the opening bars it becomes an underlying ostinato pattern that provides the background for the main theme of the festive dance. In the middle section it provides a lilting tarantella tune. Later, in the recapitulation of the opening section, it functions as a cantus firmus in long notes against the prevailing 12/8 rhythm of the dance as the piece closes on a note of abounding vitality.

The Triumph of Saint Joan Symphony is one of only a few works composed by Dello Joio after the success of *Variations, Chaconne, and Finale* that was not commissioned. It was written during the summer of 1951, at his home in Weston, Connecticut. A year earlier he had written his first opera, *The Triumph of Joan* (see chapter 9) for a student production at Sarah Lawrence College. Because of the externally imposed restrictions of the production, he did not feel that the opera represented all that he wished to say on the subject of Joan of Arc. He therefore withdrew the opera score from circulation following the initial performances, and decided to express symphonically his feelings about Joan and what her life represented. Concerning the symphony, he wrote:

> The symphony is in three movements, and the movements are subtitled "The Maid," "The Warrior," and "The Saint." Each movement is not intended to be literal, but an attempt to capture the essence of those three periods in Joan's life which seem to expand the activities of her entire life.
>
> The work has little relationship to the opera that I wrote of the same name, except for the usage of certain thematic material, but this work is completely conceived in terms of symphonic structure as it differs from operatic structure. The first movement is based on a French chanson, "La Rossignole Chi Chant," of the fifteenth century, in variation form. The second movement is martial, reaching a peak which abruptly goes into a coda which suggests the coronation of the Dauphin, Charles VII, and ends on a note of triumph and rejoicing. The last movement is somber, highly intense, closing very quietly with musical references to the theme of the first movement.[11]

The circumstances under which the symphony premiered on 5 December 1951 involved, for the second time in Dello Joio's career, Martha Graham. An article by William Mootz which appeared in *Musical America* shortly after the premiere would lead one to believe that Miss Graham had the music written expressly for her and that her dance was a smashing success.[12] However, the composer recalls the events quite differently:

I was writing it (*The Triumph of Saint Joan Symphony*) and she (Martha Graham) called me on the phone saying that she had a commission from the Louisville Symphony to do a work, and wanted to know if I would write the music. I was in the middle of this (symphony) and said, "I don't think I can do it . . ." Then I told her about what I was doing. She said, "Well could I do it?" It was to be a solo dance. I said to her that this was going to be in length about forty-five minutes" "Do you think you can sustain dancing for forty-five minutes?" She said yes. So I gave her the idea, and she took the idea to dance Joan of Arc. . . . I had the whole thing broken down into three sections—The Maid, The Warrior, and The Saint. A lot of people think it was one of her greatest works, but it was a disaster. The music received a very warm ovation, but she spent much of her time just running around the stage. It took her about two or three years and she put it into its present form (under the title *Seraphic Dialogue*) in which she didn't dance at all. She had three different dancers do the three different stages of Joan's life. [13]

Although the symphony in actuality takes only about twenty-seven minutes to perform, it is indeed symphonic in concept and scope. It does not need choreography to project its intended message. Paul Hume described it accurately when he stated, "It is romantic in concept and execution. It presents the orchestra in the Straussian tone poem manner, with heroics for all sections, and beautiful writing for the solo instruments." [14]

Dello Joio's next composition for orchestra, *Epigraph*, was commissioned by Mrs. Frederick H. Douglas of Denver, Colorado, in memory of her brother, A. Lincoln Gillespie, who died in 1950. The work was composed during the fall of 1951. Mr. Gillespie was a native Philadelphian, professor at the University of Pennsylvania, and a patron of the arts. Dello Joio had never met the man, and knew of him only what was revealed in letters from Saul Caston, conductor of the Denver Symphony, who premiered the work on 29 January 1952. For that initial performance, Dello Joio supplied this comment: "My *Epigraph* is simply a piece written to the memory of a man. It is at best a musical inscription that is conceived in terms of my own imagination as to what A. Lincoln Gillespie was like. It is musically in the form of a three part song. I did not feel compelled to write a dirgelike type of music, but music that sang, maybe roughly at times, and maybe with humor—because I suspect that is what Mr. Gillespie would have wanted." [15]

Musically, *Epigraph* is based on a four note germinal motive (DGFD) that is introduced in the opening bars. This motive then serves as the basis of the thematic material for both the A and B sections. In the A section (Pochettino piu movendo) characteristic intervals of the motive are incorporated in the extended lyrical melody played first by the upper woodwinds at figure B, with first violins dovetailing in after three bars. Motivic figures are also heard frequently in the accompanying parts. In the ensuing B section (Semplice, allegro, molto leggero) the motive and its inversion become the headpieces of themes of a sprightly character. The closing pages then provide a return to the quiet contemplative atmosphere of the beginning. As a whole, the work is modest, composed in a simple, easily comprehensible style.

The circumstances surrounding the composition of Dello Joio's Pulitzer Prize-winning composition, *Meditations on Ecclesiastes*, have already been chronicled in chapter 1, and need not be repeated here. What is needed is a close examination of the score to discover what factors contribute to its fundamental uniqueness and make it outstanding among Dello Joio's compositions.

The inspiration for both the music and the choreography was the well known passage from the book of Ecclesiastes:

> To everything there is a season, and a time to every purpose under the heaven:
> A time to be born, and a time to die; a time to plant and a time to pluck up that which is planted;
> A time to kill, and a time to heal; a time to break down and a time to build up;
> A time to weep, and a time to laugh; a time to mourn and a time to dance;
> A time to cast away stones, and a time to gather stones together; a time to embrace, and a time to refrain from embracing;
> A time to get, and a time to lose; a time to keep, and a time to cast away;
> A time to rend, and a time to sew; a time to keep silence and a time to speak;
> A time to love, and a time to hate; a time of war, and a time of peace.
>
> Eccelesiastes III, 1–8

The nature of the text suggests a theme and variations and that is exactly what resulted. "The entire work is, both choreographically and musically, a theme and variations. The choreographer used as his theme a large circle, as if to evoke the intermingled passage of time. This circle is seen repeatedly in many guises, rhythms, and dramatic shapes, always making allusions to the text . . . and its evocation of human experience."[16]

The composer used as his theme the same Gregorian melody that he used in *Variations, Chaconne, and Finale,* the "Kyrie" from the *Mass of Angels* (see example 10). Dello Joio demonstrates here and again later in his career a remarkable tenacity in his unwillingness to abandon a theme until he is satisfied that he has explored all of its possibilities for variation.

Presented with the series of antonymous experiences outlined in the text, Dello Joio used the musical elements at his disposal to create a succession of contrasting musical pictures that are unified by their derivation from the Gregorian theme. *Mediations on Ecclesiastes* consists of an introduction, the theme, and ten variations, each exploring one of the phases of human experience described in the text. The introduction draws the circle. It opens up space with the use of large intervals (open 4ths and 5ths) between the notes of the chords, and an encompassing melody in the first violins that moves with successive wide leaps in a single direction to cover a wide pitch range. The nature of the Gregorian theme is suggested with subtlety by the frequent use of rising 3ds and 5ths in the melody. The opening passage in the first violins (Eb C Bb G) could be perceived as a retrograde form of the theme (G B C D E) in minor. The cadence to G major and C major in bars 13 and 21 respectively with the subsequent flatting of the 3d of the chord evokes the contrasting sound of major and minor modes that will be exploited in subsequent variations.

The theme (. . . a time to be born . . .) contrasts vividly with Variation 1 (. . . a time to die . . .). Note in example 11 how the G-major orientation of the theme is maintained. Within the four-strand contrapuntal texture the cellos and basses play an ostinato pattern based on the first four notes of the Kyrie melody while the first violins play a melodic/rhythmic variant of the same melody. Against the parellel 3d accompanying motive of the second violins and the sustaining of the 3d of the chord by the violas, all of this is presented at a soft dynamic level to create appropriate feelings of joy and satisfaction associated with new life.

Observe the stark contrast heard in the first variation. The abrupt change from G major to E-flat minor, the loud dynamic level, and the intervalic contraction of the notes of the theme in bar 3 (first violins) all serve to create feelings of remorse. These feelings are intensified as the rising melodic line, increasing textural and rhythmic density, growing in-

Example 11. *Meditations on Ecclesiastes,* theme, ". . . a time to be born . . . ,"
bars 1–6

terval stress, and the angular line in the cellos and basses all combine to
create the climax in bar 10. The seed from which this variation grows is
the minor 2d derived from the third and fourth notes of the theme. Note
how this interval dominates the melodic writing in all parts.

Example 12. *Meditations on Ecclesiastes,* variation 1, ". . . and a time to die . . . ," bars 1–10

The contrast among the remaining variations is just as striking. In Variation 2 (. . . a time to plant, and a time to pluck up that which is planted . . .) the text obviously suggested the arpeggiated pizzicato figure that opens in the cellos. The athletic quality of the incessant eighth note rhythmic figures in the violas and second violins provides the energy necessary for the act of planting. The return of the theme to major tonality reflects the festive atmosphere of the harvest. With Variation 3 (. . . a time to kill . . .) fragments of the theme are brought forth in a highly dissonant context. The melodic contour of the first four notes of the theme is paralleled at the interval of a tritone. Heavy accents and dotted rhythms contribute extreme feelings of anger. In the fourth variation (. . . a time to heal . . .) the process of healing suggested the use of pure or perfect intervals—4ths and 5ths. Beginning in bar 20 the theme is heard in the key of D-flat major in the first violins, paralleled a fourth below by the second violins, while the accompanying figure is played by violas and cellos in parallel 5ths. The use of a lilting 6/8 meter also contributes a soothing effect. The fifth variation (. . . a time to break down, and a time to build up . . .) finds the theme at first broken up into motivic fragments and then built up again in a rising sequential passage that leads to the climax of this movement. The point of departure for the intense melodic expression of Variation 6 (. . . a time to weep and a time to mourn . . .) is the series of minor 3ds that opened the Introduction. Throughout the history of tonal music, the minor key and its most characteristic interval, the minor 3d, have been used to convey feelings of sorrow. Dello Joio capitalizes on that fact by his abundant use of that interval in both the accompanying motives and the stirring lines played by the first and second violins in counterpoint. The suggestion of dancing or jubilation often calls forth a lively rhythmic ostinato in Dello Joio's music and Variation 7 (. . . a time to dance, and a time to laugh . . .) is no exception. The accompaniment to the principal melody in the first violins is a pizzicato ostinato pattern in the cellos against off-beat pizzicato chords in the violas and second violins. Outlines of the Gregorian theme can be heard in isolated bars, normally in a contrasting mode such as the lydian. In the opening bars of Variation 8 (. . . a time to embrace and a time to refrain from embracing . . .) fragments of the theme are shared by violas and cellos while the violins engage in subtle, but effective text painting. The use of consistent contrary motion means the melodic lines are either moving toward each other (embracing) or away from each other (refrain from embracing). At bar 16 this idea becomes more brazen as the two lines engage in a passionate embrace. The first violins glide down the scale to F while the second violins soar up to meet them on the adjacent E. Following this climactic point the fragments of the opening bars return and a solo violin soars in ecstasy up to a high B as the movement closes on E major. In Variation 9 (. . . a time to hate and a time of war . . .) stress is created by conflict. Bichordal harmonies clash against one another in the opening bars. Later the contrapuntal texture results in conflicting rhythmic patterns. Repeated pitches and wild melodic leaps create agitation. Melodic direction is consistently rising until the foes exhaust themselves and feelings of stress dissolve into an attitude of reconciliation via the sustained G that connects this movement to the last. Something unexpected occurs in Variation 10 (. . . a time to love, and a time of peace . . .). Instead of a return to the Gregorian theme in its original form, as was the case in *Variations, Chaconne, and Finale,* Dello Joio employs a theme from the score of *Air Power* which was in progress at the same time. It is the melody that accompanies the safe return home after an Allied raid over Germany during World War II. Presented in a homophonic texture of extended tertain chords, the melody does not appear to be out of place because there is a logical musical connection. The stepwise contour follows exactly that of notes two through eight of the Kyrie theme which, perhaps by an unconscious choice, was the source from which the *Air Power* melody was derived.

From the outline just presented, one basic conclusion may be drawn. In creating the music of *Meditations on Ecclesiastes,* Dello Joio did not suddenly employ a new musical language. The harmonic progressions, the types of melodic motives, the rhythmic patterns, even the basic theme have all been used before. What he has done is create something new out of his familiar materials. Dello Joio is a skilled craftsman and has always been able to turn out a quality product on demand. However, one senses in this score that spark of creativity, the kind of inspiration that is the mark of a true masterwork. The enlivened rhythms, the engaging melodic turns, the seemingly spontaneous logic of the thematic relationships, the above average skill of the contrapuntal writing are all factors that contribute to the success of the work. Even the use of the time-worn device of the contrast of major and minor qualities to illustrate contrasting elements of the text somehow takes on a new meaning in the present context. One also senses that there were probably external forces at work behind the creation of this score. Just as the text and music present a study in contrasts (birth/death, love/hate, laughter/

mourning, etc.), Dello Joio's life style at this point was a study in contrasts—"I was working in two different worlds, neither of which had anything to do with the other."[17] The constant pressure under which he was working to meet the deadlines for the *Air Power* series created feelings of stress which could possibly have surfaced unconsciously while he was at work on *Meditations*. His identification with the contrasting emotional states of the men at war who appeared in the *Air Power* films could have resulted in a state of mind that had its effect on the kind of writing that went into *Meditations*. Whatever the reasons, one thing is certain; at another time and under a different set of circumstances, Dello Joio would not have written the same music that he did.

In 1957, Dello Joio selected several segments of the music he had composed for the *Air Power* series (see chapter 8) and fashioned them into a symphonic suite. The suite consists of an Introduction that presents the main theme, and three movements: 1. "Frolics of the Early Days"; 2. "Mission in the Sky"; 3. "War Scenes." The first movement divides into three sections—"Parade of the Daredevils," "Skylarking," and "Sport Meet"—which depict the daring and, from our vantage point, somewhat comical attempts at flight by the would-be aviators of the early 1900s. "Mission in the Sky" is concerned with a bombing mission over Germany during World War II. It covers the action from the alert through the takeoff, air battle, and safe return home. "War Scenes" presents six contrasting episodes, each reflecting a different effect of the war on people's lives. The main theme of the Introduction serves as a unifying force throughout the suite. It recurs in a cyclical fashion and it, as well as the homecoming theme of movement 2, is used effectively by means of thematic transformation in the second, fourth, and sixth episodes of the final movement.

A second orchestral work by Dello Joio that is based on a score originally written for television is *Scenes from the Louvre*, but this score is much more frequently heard as a transcription for band (see chapter 7). Additional orchestral works that are based on scores originally written for other media include *Five Images* for orchestra (a transcription of *Five Images* for piano), *On Stage* (a suite for small orchestra based on the ballet of the same title), and *Three Songs of Chopin* (based on the choral work of the same title). *Five Images* and *Three Songs of Chopin*, as well as three works for string orchestra—*Air for Strings* (1967), *Choreography* (1972), and *Arietta for Strings* (1978)—were written for performers in the educational sphere. All are kept within the technical and musical attainment of a good school or community orchestra. Common practice melodic, harmonic, and rhythmic procedures are the norm in each of these pieces.

The remaining works to be discussed in this chapter resulted from commissions. *Homage to Haydn* (1968) was commissioned by Miss Lily Peter of Marvel, Arkansas, for the occasion of the Arkansas Sesquicentennial in June of 1969. *Colonial Variants* and *Southern Echoes* were both commissioned for the United States Bicentennial in 1976, the former by the Farmers Bank of Wilmington, Delaware, and the latter by the Regional Metropolitan Orchestra Managers Association backed by funding from the National Endowment for the Arts.

Lily Peter not only commissioned Dello Joio to write an orchestral work; she also engaged the Philadelphia Orchestra and Eugene Ormandy to premiere the work at a series of concerts in Little Rock on 3 and 4 June 1969. When considering what to write for the occasion, Dello Joio contacted Miss Peter to inform her that he was considering using material from a work that he had recently composed for band (*Fantasies on a Theme by Haydn*; see chapter 7) which was based on a theme of Franz Joseph Haydn (1732–1809). Miss Peter wrote to Dello Joio that her great uncle, John Frederick, had copied by hand the complete manuscript of Haydn's *Creation* in London in 1809, and had arranged for the American premiere of the work in 1811 in the Central Moravian Church in Bethlehem, Pennsylvania.[18] Therefore she was delighted at the prospect of Dello Joio's work being connected with Haydn.

Fantasies on a Theme by Haydn consists of four movements, the theme followed by three fantasies (variations). In reworking this material for *Homage to Haydn*, Dello Joio fashioned the work into three movements. For the first movement he combined the material from the Theme and Fantasy 1 of *Fantasies* into a single movement that is preceded by a slow introduction of twenty-one bars, thus producing an Adagio/Allegro movement of the type that begins so many Haydn symphonies. Although there are some alterations by way of extension in the transition areas, and the material from the slow introduction is repeated in the Allegro section, there are also large blocks of material that are simply an orchestration of sections of the band score. The second and third movements are based on movements 2 and 3 respectively of *Fantasies*, and both parallel the band score very closely. The alterations are again achieved by lengthening the transition areas through extension of motivic ideas. Although both *Homage to Haydn* and *Fantasies on a Theme by Haydn* are based on the same thematic material, and the individual movements parallel each other quite closely, both works are true to their respective medium, and the end result in both instances is very satisfying.

Colonial Variants was also premiered by the Philadelphia Orchestra under Eugene Ormandy at a series of concerts given 27, 28, and 29 May 1976 in Wilmington, Delaware. These concerts marked the completion of a major Wilmington Bicentennial project, the reopening of the newly restored Grand Opera House as Delaware's new Center for the Performing Arts. Dello Joio subtitled the work "13 Profiles of the Original Colonies, Based on an Ancient Tune." The tune in question is the familiar "In dulci jubilo" which is also encountered in *Variants on a Medieval Tune* and *Scenes from the Louvre* (see chapter 7). The tune is stated straightway in the Introduction (Andante semplice) in the key of C by the bassoon and English horn with elaboration by the strings and other woodwinds. It is then followed by a series of thirteen variations, each representing one of the original colonies. The variations progress through the complete cycle of fifths (allowing each of the twelve chromatic tones to serve as the tonal center of one variation), with the final variant (Massachusetts) closing in a choralelike manner in C major. Variations 6 and 7 (North and South Carolina) are connecting, and are in the pivotal key of F-sharp and G-flat. The Carolinas are also the only variants in this work that relate to *Variants on a Medieval Tune*, the material being a reworking of variation 3 of the band score which was composed in 1963. Dello Joio stated that *Colonial Variants* "is in no way to be thought of as programmatic; it is an exercise in structural musical fancies and impressions, with no literal connotations."[19]

Southern Echoes was premiered by the Savannah Symphony on 22 January 1977, George Trautwein conducting. It is a dance suite in three movements that comments not on any specifics, but on the composer's understanding of the Southern climate, folkways, nearness of the people to their land, and the gentle leisurely tempo of their life style. The leisurely tempo is reflected in the first two movements—Andante calmo, and Adagio. The Allegro finale is a spirited rondo.

The opening movement is a through-composed structure in which all the thematic material is derived from two chords stated near the beginning of the movement. Dello Joio's use of a germinal motive in many of his works for chorus and orchestra has already been noted. Here the seed is reduced to a chord. The material unfolds gradually as first only the chord is stated, then a short motive, and later a full-fledged theme. Note the relationships in the example below.

Example 13. *Southern Echoes,* movement 1

The Adagio movement is based on a lyrical theme which, in an enlivened rhythmic transformation, becomes the principle theme of the rondofinale as well. The subsidiary themes of the rondo are both diatonic C-major tunes, the first a martial trumpet call, and the second an expansive lyrical idea. The language of *Southern Echoes,* with its use of mildly dissonant to consonant harmonies and diatonically based themes reflects Dello Joio's tendency in his later years to react to contemporary avant-garde practices by clinging even more tenaciously to traditional musical values. The same may be said of *Ballabili* (1981), a set of dances for orchestra that are based on the *Concert Variations* for piano of 1980.

4

Concertos

The concerto is a genre to which Dello Joio devoted considerable attention during his student years and those immediately following, but with two notable exceptions has neglected since that time. *Concertino* for flute and strings (1939), *Concertino in Stilo Classico* for piano and orchestra (1940), and Concerto for two pianos and orchestra (1941) were all composed during his years as a graduate student at Juilliard. The *Concertino* for flute and strings and the Concerto for two pianos and orchestra were both premiered at student composition concerts at Juilliard, the former on 11 May 1940, and the latter on 14 May 1942. *Concertino in Stilo Classico* was premiered on 4 April 1941 by the New York Chamber Orchestra with Vivian Rifkin, pianist. *Concertino* for harmonica and orchestra (1944) was written for the harmonica player John Sebastian, who performed the work frequently on tour. The Concerto for harp and orchestra (1945) was commissioned by Edna Phillips, harpist with the Philadelphia Orchestra. According to Dello Joio she never performed it, presumably because she did not like it. The premiere was given by Carlos Salzedo with the Little Orchestra Society on 3 October 1947. Dello Joio wrote *Tre Ricercare* for piano and orchestra (1946) for himself, and he premiered the work with George Szell and the New York Philharmonic on 19 December 1946. *Concertante* for clarinet and orchestra (1949) was composed as a commissioned work for clarinetist Artie Shaw who premiered the work on 22 May 1949 at Chautauqua, New York. A version of this work for clarinet and piano by the composer was published in 1955. Since 1948, only two concertos have come from Dello Joio's pen. *Ballad of the Seven Lively Arts* for piano and orchestra (1957) was composed because he needed a vehicle in which he could be featured as a performer on the television program "Profile of a Composer." *Fantasy and Variations* for piano and orchestra (1961) was commissioned by the Baldwin Piano Company on the occasion of its one hundredth anniversary. The world premiere was given by the Cincinnati Symphony Orchestra on 9 March 1962 with Max Rudolf conducting, and Lorin Hollander, pianist. It was subsequently recorded by Mr. Hollander for RCA Victor with the Boston Symphony under Eric Leinsdorf.

The stylistic development that is evident in these concertos parallels that found in the orchestral works—movement from complexity to simplicity in terms of melodic construction, and movement towards a more economical use of thematic material either through variations or development from a thematic cell. The concertos dating from the Juilliard years reveal a preoccupation with the composition of well conceived melodies. Contrast is achieved by the use of contrasting melodic ideas, usually one rhythmic and energetic, and the other lyrical and cantabile (examples 14 and 15).

Example 14. *Concertino* for flute and strings, theme 1 from movement 1

Example 15. *Concertino* for flute and strings, theme 2 from movement 1

These ideas are typically presented in ABA' form. Thematic material is extended through modified repetition, and there is some use of imitative and canonic treatment in the second movement of *Concertino* for flute and strings. The Concerto for two pianos and orchestra is noteworthy because it is the first composition in which Dello Joio employed the liturgical theme "Kyrie" from the *Mass of Angels* (see the discussion of *Variations, Chaconne, and Finale* in chapter 3). It is the theme of the first movement in which it is heard in a series of modified repetitions, but is it not subjected to the formal variation procedure that it receives in *Variations, Chaconne, and Finale* and Sonata no. 3 for piano.

The Concerto for harp and orchestra contains a set of variations, the first time that Dello Joio employed this formal procedure in one of his compositions. The first movement (Adagio) consists of a theme and ten variations which are preceded by a brief introduction and followed by a short postlude. An original eight-bar theme divided symmetrically into two four-bar phrases shows an approach to form that is rooted in the eighteenth century, yet the melodic content, with its free use of the twelve tones within the octave, is very much of the twentieth century. The harmonic language which is tinged with dissonance throughout is also a product of the present era. The variation procedures are, like the formal structure of the theme, rooted in traditional practice. Throughout the first four variations the technique is similar to that of the eighteenth century passacaglia in which the theme itself remains unaltered (except for color changes produced by varying the instrumentation) while the surrounding material undergoes changes in harmony and texture with each variation. In the remaining variations the theme itself undergoes modification by means of melodic alteration and fragmentation.

The Allegro finale is a sectional form (ABA′B′) which alternates passages of percussive, rhythmic vitality with passages emphasizing lyrical melody. The harp is prominent throughout the movement as the contrasting passages allow the instrument a wide range of expressive possibilities from subtle innuendo to bravura passage-work that leads to an exciting close on D major.

Despite the title, the *Tre Ricercare* is in effect a three-movement piano concerto. There is little in the score that would point to the imitative (contrapuntal) ricercar as a model. Dello Joio evidently had in mind a type of organ ricercar characterized by free-voice writing, cadential coloraturas, and passages in toccata style that were often intended to display the virtuosity of the performer. The brilliant, athletic passages in the outer movements allow the keyboard player ample opportunity for dazzling display of dexterity. The calm middle movement is a mood-setting piece that provides a momentary break in the mounting tension. Each movement features a different musical element. In the first movement it is harmony as the orchestra progresses rapidly through a kaleidoscopic display of chord changes while the basic thematic material is presented by the piano in the alternating pattern of a rondo. The second movement focuses on a melodic idea as the third theme from the first movement is transformed into a lyrical idea that becomes the theme for a set of variations.[1] The focus of the third movement is on rhythm. A single rhythmic pattern (2/4 ♫ 𝄾 ♫♫ ♪ ♫ | ♪ 𝄾 ♫♫ ♪) is the unifying element, but more important is the composer's ingenuity at subdividing the beat. During the course of the movement there are a minimum of fifty different means of organizing the rhythm of a 2/4 bar. The syncopated rhythm of the theme, played first by the piano, then taken up by the trumpets and trombones against fluttering, syncopated figuration in the piano, provides a kind of infectious excitement that is characteristic of the finales of many of Dello Joio's instrumental works.

With the *Concertante* for clarinet and orchestra one encounters a definite advancement in compositional technique, and a change of attitude as well. Having been written soon after the *Variations, Chaconne, and Finale* for orchestra and the *Variations and Capriccio* for violin and piano (see chapter 5), this work reveals the kind of mastery of development and variation technique that is evident in those works. In terms of his attitude toward his own composition, Dello Joio had advanced beyond the point of being concerned about being modern. Concerning the *Concertante* he said: "This is one of my earlier works that has satisfied me. It is one of the works that made Hindemith aware of the lyrical quality of my work and he said that 'You are a lyricist by nature, don't do anything to disturb that or try to be consciously modern for its own sake. Just let yourself sing.' This piece does that, and does it well. I allowed myself to have a long line in terms of a lyric statement whereas before, I tended to chop it off when I felt I was getting too Romantic."[2]

The advancement in compositional technique is immediately obvious in the *Concertante*. Instead of achieving contrast with the use of a polythematic structure, Dello Joio now chooses to explore the differing possibilities for emotional expression inherent within a single theme. In the first movement the theme is set in a slow-fast-slow sectional form while being subjected to continual development melodically and rhythmically. Dello Joio's choice of theme shows the movement toward simplicity alluded to earlier in this chapter. Compare the brevity and simple diatonic structure of example 16 with examples 14 and 15.

Example 16. *Concertante* for clarinet and orchestra, movement 1, bars 1–2

His concern now is not with the theme as an end in itself, but with its potential for manipulation through developmental and variation procedures.

This same concern is evident in the theme and variations that comprise the second movement. With the exception of the two modal inflections (E♭ in bar 3 and F♯ in bar 4) the theme is constructed solely from the notes of the G mixolydian scale.

Example 17. *Concertante* for clarinet and orchestra, movement 2, bars 1–6

Note also the symmetry of its form—a four-bar phrase dividing into two-bar motives—and the economy of means in its construction. The entire theme is simply an extension of the first three notes (G A D). Bar 2 is a repetition of this motive with embellishment. Bar 3 contains a sequential repetition of the same motive with the fifth inverted to a fourth, and bar 4 is a repetition of bar 1 with slightly different embellishment. Within the two-voice contrapuntal texture over a tonic pedal, even the accompanying figure (G F# D E F, referred to as figure A for purposes of this discussion) is derived from bar 4 of the theme. During the course of the variations, Dello Joio's penchant for ostinato patterns is evident as he often seizes either figure A or a fragment of the theme and uses it repetitively while the theme undergoes moderate and sometimes radical transformation. Figure A, for example, is the underlying ostinato for variations 1 and 3 while the retrograde of notes nine through eleven of the theme serves the same purpose in variation 2. Variations 4 and 5 do not employ the ostinato as such, but variation 5 is based on a melodic figure that is derived by compressing together the alternate minor and major triads implied by bars 2 and 4 of the theme.

The concertato element implied by the title is achieved by alternating thematic segments between the clarinet and the accompanying instruments. There is ample room for expression by the soloist as the extreme ranges of the clarinet are explored (chalumeau in variations 3 and 4, altissimo in variation 5) in a variety of articulatory styles—legato, tenuto, marcato, and staccato. Wide, angular melodic leaps, and unfamiliar scalar contingencies resulting from modal and pentatonic scales, could provide some technical difficulties for all but the most accomplished clarinetists. Rhythmic difficulties include syncopation, sudden shifts of accent within a cross rhythmic context, and unconventional application of rests. However, the aesthetic satisfaction derived from the performance of a work of this calibre should make any difficulties encountered well worth overcoming.

Ballad of the Seven Lively Arts is a concerto in one movement that contains an abundance of themes all related by their common dependence on the interval of the minor third. This interval is the basis of a thematic cell (Eb C Bb G C A) that is outlined in the first three bars which are played slowly. The music then launches immediately into an energetic section in which several short motivic figures are stated and developed. A modified repetition of the thematic cell (bars 43-44) separates this opening section from the Allegro section which follows. Here the minor third is incorporated into two cantabile themes. The ensuing development of these themes further exploits the minor third with abundant use of percussion. A slow lyrical section (bars 142–63) introduces two additional themes, the second a joyous Gregorian melody (example 19) featuring chimes, bells, and brass. The energetic motives of the opening sections then return in varied form to bring the work to its close. Like *Tre Ricercare* which Dello Joio also wrote for himself to perform, *Ballad of the Seven Lively Arts* features lively, syncopated rhythms and dazzling leaps over the keyboard in order to display the composer's own manner of virtuosity.

Fantasy and Variations for piano and orchestra is not only Dello Joio's crowning achievement in the concerto genre; it is one of his most perfect compositions in any genre. As with *Meditations on Ecclesiastes,* it is not the use of new material that makes this work unique, but the remarkable skill with which he employs familiar material. *Fantasy and Variations* is both architectonic and evolutionary. Within the familiar variations form, each stage of the work evolves from, and is dependent on, one of the previous stages. The entire work is based on a four note cell (G F# B C), and that cell is based on a single interval, the minor second. By taking the final step back to the origin of this evolutionary process, we arrive at the simplest of all musical organisms— a single note, and that is how this composition begins. Now a single note is totally noncommittal. It is not until that note is sounded together with or in succession with at least one other note that it has implications for future events. The movement from F to Gb on the first beat of bar 1 is therefore highly significant. It defines the character of the thematic cell and consequently the personality of the entire composition.

The *Fantasy,* which is in three-part form (Adagio, Allegro, Adagio), begins with the piano quietly exploring some of the implications of the thematic cell. The characteristic interval (minor second) is first expanded (bars 1–2) and then inverted to the major seventh (bar 3). The orchestra suddenly interrupts with a forte statement of the bichord F#/C (the two triads being built on the second and fourth notes of the cell) which leads to the first complete statement of the cell by the tympani (bar 8). The piano enters again, first with chromatic lines in contrary motion, then with the notes of the cell combined into a four-note chord—arpeggiated ninths first, then blocks of minor seconds—which culminate in a second statement of the cell (bar 13). The remainder of the Adagio is based on material already presented. The minor second becomes the basis for sequential passages such as that played by the piano in bar 18, and scalar passages based on the locrian scale which begins with a half step. The

Allegro section begins in the orchestra with the cellular structure reordered (B C F# G) and explores further permutations of the original cell. The piano is featured in bravura passagework supported by lively figurations in the orchestra. The return of the Adagio is brief and closes quietly on the F with which the *Fantasy* began, a gesture that leaves the listener in doubt concerning the tonality. The thematic cell itself is noncommittal with respect to tonality, and the fact that the *Fantasy* neither begins nor ends with one of the notes of the cell does not clarify the issue.

Following the *Fantasy* are six variations, each based on the four-note cell, but each with its own individual character. Variation 1 (Adagio) explores further the ideas presented in the first eight bars of the *Fantasy*. The orchestra begins variation 2 (Allegro scherzando) with a new variant of the cell. After only a few bars, however, the piano takes over and assumes the dominant role with much virtuosic display. Variation 3 (Andante amabile) is characterized by a lilting rhythm in duple compound meter as yet another permutation of the cell is heard in the orchestra while the piano sings freely above. The piano opens the fourth variation with a passage of three bars culminating in vigorous trills on the notes of the original cell. The orchestra then joins in as two participants engage in a brilliant interplay of material derived from the cell. A new ordering of the notes of the cell opens variation 5 (Adagio mesto) as the piano and orchestra answer each other in an antiphonal manner. Variation 6 (Allegro gioioso) is in a whirling 12/8 rhythm that is characteristic of the finales of many of Dello Joio's instrumental works (see *New York Profiles* and *Concertante for Wind Instruments*). The ordering of the notes of the cell is the same as that of variation 3 in the opening bars. Piano and orchestra cooperate vigorously in bringing the work to a brilliant conclusion on C major. Dello Joio's arrival at this point is accomplished in a characteristic (for him) manner. The F-sharp and C-major triads (from bar 7 of the *Fantasy*) rival one another for the predominant position with C major finally emerging as the winner.

With the composition of *Fantasy and Variations*, Dello Joio achieved a mastery of compositional technique that he had not achieved before and has not surpassed since. Only a master composer could develop a lengthy composition such as this out of a brief four-note cell. The use of a thematic cell is not new in this work. *Concert Music* for orchestra (1944) is the first example of its use (he called it a motto in that work) in Dello Joio's work. In that early work, however, the motto functioned more like a signpost that recurs periodically to remind the listener that he/she is still on the same path. In the 1950s the use of the thematic cell became increasingly common in his works. *Song of the Open Road* and the opera *The Ruby* are notable examples, and in these works the cell with its various permutations is responsible for a much greater percentage of the musical content than was the case with *Concert Music*. However, in no other composition by Dello Joio does a single four-note cell permeate the entire score to the extent that it does in *Fantasy and Variations*. Every new idea presented in the score evolves from an idea presented earlier, and all of the ideas can be traced back to a single original idea—the cell.

5

Chamber Music

> My leanings as a composer always take me to the big forms of music—symphonies, choral works, opera, ballet—I have never been tempted to write a string quartet. Whenever I sit down at my desk with new musical ideas, they always turn out big.[1]

NDJ

Taken at face value, the quotation above would indicate that Dello Joio's chamber works were not the result of an inner conviction or instinctive urge to write for the small ensemble. Although it is risky to draw such a conclusion on the basis of a statement taken out of context, an examination of the circumstances surrounding each of his compositions in this medium will reveal that with the exception of a few youthful indiscretions from his student years, all of his chamber works were written at the request of a specific individual (usually a concert artist and friend of the composer) for performance on a specific occasion. Another observation worth mentioning is the fact that the majority of the chamber works were written during the early years of his career when he was striving for recognition, and he certainly would not have declined the opportunity to write for an accomplished artist who intended to perform his music. By the late forties, Dello Joio was firmly established as one of America's first rank composers, and following the completion of *Variations and Cappricio* in 1948, he did not write for this medium again until 1963. During those intervening years his primary attention was focused on the big forms—orchestra music, opera, ballet, and music for television and films. Several chamber works date from the period when Dello Joio was a student at the Institute of Musical Art and the Juilliard Graduate School.

Among them are a Sonata for cello and piano (1937), two sonatas for violin and piano (one in 1937 and one in 1938), a Quartet for four bassoons (1937), a Trio for piano, violin, and cello (1937), *Colloquy* for violin and piano (1938), a Quartet for flute, oboe, clarinet, and bassoon (1939), and a Trio for clarinet, French horn, and bassoon (1940). None of these works are published, and with the exception of the Sonata for cello and piano and *Colloquy*, the location of the scores remains a mystery. Recital programs found in the composer's collection of memorabilia indicate that all of them were performed on programs at Juilliard which featured compositions by resident students. The Sonata for cello and piano was performed on at least two other occasions. Sterling Hunkins performed it with the composer at the piano at the MacDowell Club on 17 March 1941 and George Neikrug played it in a New York recital on 17 March 1943. Dello Joio later dismissed these works as unimportant and withdrew them from circulation.

The earliest published chamber work is the *Fantasia on a Gregorian Theme* for violin and piano (1941–42) which was written for Eudice Shapiro to premiere at a Town Hall concert on 1 April 1942. Originally entitled *Ite Missa Est*,[2] the work is based on two of the Gregorian melodies that are sung to the concluding phrase of the Roman Catholic Mass. The first is the chant used from the Paschal Vigil till Easter Saturday inclusive (example 18),[3] and the second is performed for "Feasts of the first class." (example 19)[4].

Example 18. "Ite Missa Est" from Paschal Vigil to Easter Sunday inclusive

Example 19. "Ite Missa Est" for Feasts of the first class

Therefore the work is in actuality a fantasia on two themes. The first, based on the first four pitches of example 18, is stated in octaves by the violin alone, and then the piano joins with open fifths that set the mood for the entire composition. Although the second theme (example 19) is

anticipated by a melodic variant in bar 25, it is not stated outright until bar 45 where the violin plays it in C major over supporting chords by the piano. The violin and piano alternate in weaving elaborations about the themes in their original and varied forms. The modal coloring and spaciousness of the work is reminiscent of the English composer Ralph Vaughan Williams (1872–1958), but the harmonization and melodic treatment is unmistakably that of Dello Joio.

A Sextet for three recorders and string trio (9–19 May 1943) was commissioned by Harold Newman, president of the American Recorder Society. The work is scored for soprano, alto, and tenor recorders, violin, viola, and cello.[5] Writing for such a combination of instruments is a rarity today, and it was even more unusual in 1943, when the practice of performing on Renaissance and Baroque instruments was not so widespread as it has become in recent years. Dello Joio's talents were equal to the task. His feeling for modality that is a manifestation of his knowledge of Gregorian chant is evident in the compositional style of this piece. Composed in four contrasting movements, the work shows idiomatic writing for all instruments employed. The first movement is even based on a cantus firmus—"World Farewell, Put Me To Rest"—a fact that further relates the composition to the music of the remote past.

The Trio for flute, cello and piano (13 December 1943–9 January 1944) was written for the LeRoy, Foster, Scholz Trio. It was premiered 1 March 1944 at Town Hall, and was recorded for Concert Hall Society Records in 1947, the first work of Dello Joio's to be heard in recorded form. The Trio is in three movements, each of which follow a three part pattern of tonal emphasis in which the tonal area of the opening bars returns at the end after intervening areas of tonal contrast. Although the music contains the same basic gravitational pulls of traditional common practice harmony, the melodies, which are not tied to the conventions of major and minor scales nor to the conventional meeting points of the common triad, pass through dissonant proximities with one another on the way to their logical destination.

The first movement, in rocking 6/8 meter, begins with a trill-like sixteenth note figure by the flute which serves an important motivic function throughout the movement. The principle theme is a seven-bar legato melody first played by the piano beginning on the keynote B-flat (bar 12) and imitated on the dominant by the cello (bar 22). There follows a rich succession of melodic and rhythmic variants that lead to a section of reiterated sixteenth-note pitches (bar 98) in which the accumulation of dissonance and rising melodic line lead to a forceful climax (bar 111), after which the tension dissipates and the movement comes to a quiet close in which thematic fragments are heard from the flute and cello while the piano repeats softly the sixteenth note pattern of the previous section.

The second movement is an expressive Adagio in which the composer makes skillful use of its opening motive—the decending minor second. This interval governs the melodic and harmonic structure of the entire movement. Chromatic movement is an integral part of each of the melodic lines, and chromatic voice-leading is heard frequently in the chord progressions of the piano. Following the implications of the half step motive, the principal areas of tonal emphasis are E and E-flat, and the exploitation of the half step difference between major and minor chords provides a subtle blending of the colors of major and minor modes.

The energetic third movement is related to the second by the fact that it is also based on the exploitation of a single interval. The upward leap of a minor third from F-sharp to A by both cello and flute supported by a one bar rhythmic figure (♪♪ ♪♪ ♪♪   ) that incorporates this same interval, not only defines the tonality (F# minor), but also provides the building block from which the entire musical fabric is constructed. The movement consists of five sections (ABCDA′) which are contrasting in key, melodic idea, rhythmic pattern, and texture, but all are unified by the strategic use of the minor third. Following the implications now of the minor third motive, Dello Joio maintains tonal ambiguity by the juxtaposition of notes and chords in such a way that major and relative minor can make equal claim as the principal tonality. The penultimate section is notable for its use of an unusual double stop glissando for the cello that is accomplished by sliding the fingers downward after the string has been plucked. The movement ends with a brilliant return to F-sharp, closing finally on F-sharp major as the flute moves chromatically upward from A to A-sharp, providing an enharmonic tonal link with the B-flat which was the keynote of the first movement.

Duo Concertato for cello and piano (1944) was written for Janos Scholz, the cellist in the above mentioned trio, who premiered the work on 15 October 1944. It is a single movement work in which the principal and central section (Allegro animato) achieves considerable rhythmic propulsion by the use of assymetric rhythmic groupings, implied polymeter, and shifting accents. The cantilena of the cello is used to good effect in the opening and closing sections which contain sustained passages with a high degree of emotional tension. As in the third movement of the Trio for flute, cello, and piano, the interval of the third plays a key role in the melodic and harmonic structure. The tonal center for the outer sections is C major while the third related keys of A-flat and E combine as the focal points of harmonic interest in the central section. A mark of Dello Joio's melodic writing is his use of scale patterns from more than one key in the construction of his melodies. Here the principle melody is constructed of notes of the A-flat major scale in such a way as to suggest the relative minor (F minor) at times. Another factor that contributes to the vagueness of key feeling is the conspicuous absence of the leading tone at points where its presence would confirm the tonality. Note in example 20 that the cello melody outlines the A-flat major triad in bars 48–49, and the F-minor triad in bar 50, but neither G nor E, which would confirm one key or the other, is heard in the melody or the accompaniment before the melody moves briefly into the area of E major in bar 51. The obscurity that results from this very free association of modes combines with the rhythmic treatment to give the work its mark of contemporaneity, yet the fact that the modes associated are the time-honored ones of earlier periods give the music strong ties to past tradition.

Example 20. *Duo Concertato,* bars 48–52

Variations and Capriccio for violin and piano (1–9 June 1948) was written at the request of the Cuban violinist Angel Reyes who had heard Dello Joio's third piano sonata and asked the composer to create a work for him to perform on his European tour during the spring of 1949. Reyes premiered the work at Carnegie Hall on 14 December 1948, with the composer at the piano.

The theme for the set of variations is a quiet, pastoral statement, sixteen bars in length, for piano alone. It devides into three sections—tonic (bar 1), dominant (bar 6), and tonic (bar 12). The middle section incorporates the notes of the "Ite Missa Est" motive shown in example 19. The six variations are written in a variety of meters and moods ranging from calm and serene to joyful and brilliant. Variation 1, for violin alone, is marked Semplice (simple, unaffected). The theme is manipulated by inversion and alteration of intervals, but the rhythm and basic melodic outline are clearly recognizable. Staccato articulation and angular melodic motion in a quick 3/8 meter give the second variation a lively, energetic character, and the relationship to the theme is much more tenuous. Piano and violin share equally in the presentation of the material with pizzicato being the primary mode of articulation for the violin. The brilliant third variation manipulates the notes of the "Ite Missa Est" motive, but closes by quoting the first five notes of the theme. The moderate fourth variation is a lilting 6/8 in which the violin plays a lyrical melody that emphasizes the first three notes of the theme. The piano occasionally plays thematic material in this variation, but is more often relegated to a supporting role. Variation 5 springs from jazz. It has a striking resemblance to variation 3 of the first movement of Dello Joio's third piano sonata (see chapter 6). It employs the same kind of propulsive rhythmic figures that come suddenly to a halt with a rest on the beat. While it has only a slight resemblance to the theme of the present work, it has a close relationship to the "Kyrie" theme used in the Sonata no. 3 for piano and *Variations, Chaconne, and Finale* (see example 10). A warmly sung cantilena on the violin that is closely related to the original theme of the present work rounds out the set of variations.

By way of transition, the *Capriccio* begins with a muted solo on the violin. The Vivo e giocoso (lively and humorous) section which follows moves with great rhythmic drive. The opening violin motive is related to the theme of the set of variations as it ascends first a fourth and then a fifth (the original sequence was a fifth followed by a fourth). The tempo slows a bit in the middle of the movement to allow for reminiscence of the "Ite Missa Est" motive (bar 68). At the close the muted solo from the beginning of the present movement returns, followed by references to the principle motives of the *Capriccio* and the original theme of the set of variations. The work as a whole shows a composer with keen imagination and inventiveness. Judging by the richness of ideas in the present work, which followed closely the creation of *Variations, Chaconne, and Finale* and the third piano sonata, it would appear that Dello Joio found in the variations form ample scope for his creative imagination. It is a form in which he is very comfortable, and it has served him well ever since.

In the early sixties the Ford Foundation initiated a Concert Artists Program to assist young performing artists who possessed demonstrated potential for a concert career in developing their talents and expanding their repertoire. One of the conditions that had to be met by those artists who received stipends under this program was that they must perform a composition by an American composer that was written specifically for them. As a consequence of this stipulation, the young concert violinist Sidney Harth asked Dello Joio to write a composition for him. Dello Joio accepted the commission, and the result was *Colloquies,* a concert suite for violin and piano which he composed in 1963. Harth premiered the work on 6 February 1964. Having just completed his first brief essay in twelve-tone writing (*Night Song* for piano, see chapter 6), Dello Joio decided to explore the technique further in *Colloquies.* The outcome was the most austere, highly dissonant work ever to come from the composer's pen. The suite is in six short movements all of which are based on the twelve-tone row shown in example 21.

Example 21. *Colloquies,* twelve-tone row

The opening movement (Lento expressivo) serves as an introduction that presents the thematic material on which the remaining movements are based. The various forms of the row are presented in the following order: original (O); inversion (I); retrograde (R); retrograde inversion (RI); and retrograde. The first six tones of the row are sounded in pairs on the keyboard with the dampers held open until all six are heard simultaneously. This is followed by the melodic presentation of tones 1–10 which are split between violin and piano. A second chord is built up in the same manner as the first as tones 7–12 are interjected in pairs before the melodic presentation of the row is completed by the violin. The practice of constructing chords out of successive notes of the row is not strictly adhered to beyond this point in the composition. The angular melodic contour that results from octave displacement and splitting the melody between the two instruments combines with irregular rhythmic placement of the tones to make it difficult to follow the progression of the notes in the row without considerable advance study.

In the second movement (Allegro molto e leggero) the rapid quarter note pulse, disjunct motion, persistent dissonance, and staccato articulation combine to produce a highly agitated effect. The first ten bars utilize tones 1–6 and 9 and 10 exclusively in both melody and accompaniment. Succeeding sections present transposed fragments of the row in I, RI, and O forms. The third movement (adagio mesto) is similar in character and mood to the first. It explores further transpositions of the row in both fragmented and complete form. An interesting compositional technique is used in bars 70–73. Piano and violin begin simultaneous presentations of the row in R form, the former at the tenth transposition (ten semitones above the original starting note), and the later at the third transposition. After the third note has been reached, the two instruments switch transpositions, and the piano continues the row in the third transposition while the violin continues in the tenth transposition.

Movement 4 (Presto spumante) relies on disjunct motion, dissonance, and disjointed rhythmic patterns to produce a highly animated effect. A complete statement of the row in O form is played by the violin beginning in bar 98. The rest of the movement is either freely composed or uses transposed fragments of the row. Dello Joio's skill at creating interesting and varied subdivisions of the bar is evident in this movement as the eighth note groupings and accentuation are constantly shifting.

A play on the interval of a second is combined with fragments of the row in its various forms to create the slow, tranquil fifth movement. Very economical use is made of the material at hand. The contents of the movement are revealed in the first six bars.

Further play on the interval of a second is heard in the final movement (Molto animato, con ruvidezza) as major seconds are heard almost constantly in the accompaniment while melodic emphasis is on the ninth in the violin part. Actually this interval is of greater importance in the construction of this movement than the row itself which is heard only once (bar 228, violin). Emphasis is placed on the same type of disjunct motion, dissonance, and primarily staccato articulation that were present in movements 2 and 4.

Although Dello Joio has shown great skill and imagination in his manipulation of the material in *Colloquies*, judgment of its aesthetic qualities still must be rendered on the basis of its aural effect on the listener. For while the analytical process of tracing a twelve-note row through its various octave and rhythmic displacements on the printed page provides the same sort of pleasure as finding one's way through a maze, aural recognition of these same events is often an impossibility for all but the most highly skilled listeners. While it is entirely possible to construct a twelve-tone row and use it in such a way that it is easily recognizable (as Dello Joio did in "The Lion House"), the composer has not done so in this case. A composition such as *Colloquies* must be appreciated or not appreciated because of the totality of its effect, not because of the recognition or lack thereof of a specific sequence of pitches. When the work is considered from that perspective, it is unquestionably successful. Even though it is in a language that is unusual for Dello Joio, its communication is direct, and the emotional effect on the listener is profound.

Bagatelles for harp (1969) was commissioned for the first International Harp Competition by the Hartt College of Music, University of Hartford. Unlike *Colloquies*, this work is in traditional Dello Joio style. In the first movement (Andante affettuoso) a chantlike B-flat aeolian melody combines with the frequent use of parallel fourths and fifths to impart an archaic quality. The joyful second movement depends on lively polymetric rhythmic patterns and colorful harmonic progressions for its effect. Melody is not an important element in this movement or in the calm third movement which exploits the colorful and sonorous effects that are unique to this instrument. The use of graduated dynamics, progressive and regressive dissonance, and changing melodic direction causes an ebb and flow that is somewhat impressionistic in effect.

The Developing Flutist, a suite for flute and piano (1972) and *Three Essays* for B♭ clarinet and piano (1974) were both written at the suggestion of the publisher for performers in the educational sphere. *The Developing Flutist* is cast in four movements: 1. Improviso; 2. Canon; 3. Aria; and 4. Scherzo. The Improviso is a brief improvisational passage for the flute over sustained dissonant chords from the piano that announces the thematic material for the Canon. The Canon divides into two subsections. The first (bars 1–16) is a strict three-voice canon at the octave based on a twelve-tone row. The second (bars 17–34) is a two-voice canon based on a new twelve-tone row. The middle section (bars 35–45) is based on a new point of imitation that is entirely diatonic (A minor/C major), a notable contrast to the highly chromatic twelve-tone sections. The melody of the Aria is based on the free association of the twelve tones around a tonal center of C. It is carried by the flute throughout while the piano provides support via a chromatically descending ground bass pattern that begins in bar 13. The Scherzo is based on a four-note motive announced by the flute in the first bar. The melody is freely expanded with the motive incorporated at strategic points. As in the second movement, contrast is provided by a subsidiary theme that is pandiatonic in nature. These are well conceived pieces that, even though written with the developing flutist in mind, should provide sufficient musical interest to warrant programming by the professional performer. The same may be said of *Three Essays* which consists of three contrasting movements, the second of which is identical to the Aria from the *The Developing Flutist*.

Lyric Fantasies for viola and string orchestra (or string quintet) was commissioned for violist Michael Tree, and premiered on 23 February 1975. In the two contrasting movements of this work, Dello Joio continues the practice of alternating highly chromatic sections with passages that are almost completely diatonic. The first movement begins with an Adagio section that employs a constant quarter note pulse while the meter changes at irregular intervals in time. This alternates with a section in 6/8 meter marked Amabile (amiable) to form an ABA'B'A" pattern. Actually the A sections serve as introduction, interlude, and postlude to the B sections in which the principle thematic material is presented. The material in the A section is governed by the interval of a fourth as quartal harmony accompanies melodic movement that often outlines a fourth chord. Tritonal relationships are heard in bars 18–24 where the C-major triad is juxtaposed to the G*b* (F-sharp) triad.

The Amabile section offers fine lyrical lines for the viola while the first violin in the ensemble is only slightly less important as a melodic instrument. Tonal organization is characterized by a practice that has already been discussed in this chapter—the exploitation of the close relationship between major and minor. In the B section the keys involved are G major and E minor, whereas in the B' section they are C major and A minor. Just as the painter blends two primary colors to create a secondary color, Dello Joio here blends the qualities of major and minor together in such a way that a new individual quality emerges. This same blending process is applied to the harmonic language, which possesses an individual quality because of the use of complex chords that are constructed by combining simple chords. The chord in bar 113 is a good example. From the bottom up it is spelled G C F A D. The bottom three notes form a fourth chord, the middle three a major triad, and the top three a minor triad. These three distinct chord qualities combine to form a new chord in which G functions as the root.

The second movement is related to the first by the use of a common motive (see bars 87–89 and 110–12) of the respective movements). It begins with an introduction (Allegro con spiritoso) which emphasizes the tritone in sustained chords underneath nervously repeated sixteenth notes by the viola. The main body of the movement (Allegro gioioso) begins in bar 32 with a Stravinskian passage of percussive, dissonant chords with shifting accent. The viola continues in agitated style until bar 64 where the agitation is transformed into tranquility by the use of a lyrical C-major theme in imitation by viola and violin. Following the presentation of this theme, the remainder of the movement is developmental with the material derived from the introduction, the main theme, and the thematic motive borrowed from the first movement.

In 1978, Dello Joio reworked the material from *Lyric Fantasies* into a piece for chamber orchestra entitled *Concertante*. This version follows the same format as the earlier work, but does not employ the solo viola.

The most recent chamber work to come from Dello Joio's pen is the Sonata for trumpet and piano (1979). Commissioned by the International Trumpet Guild, the work was premiered by Armando Ghitalla with James Winn at the piano at the 1979 ITG Conference at Arizona State University. David Hickman, ITG president, stated: "I (and most people, I think) have considered there to be only four truly outstanding sonatas for trumpet and piano—those by Paul Hindemith, Peter Maxwell Davies, Kent Kennan, and Halsey Stevens. . . . The Dello Joio Sonata will most likely take its place with the four outstanding sonatas . . . mentioned, making the total now five."[6]

This being his first work for trumpet, Dello Joio put his familiar materials to work to create a truly outstanding composition. The Sonata consists of three movements, a Theme and three variations, a lyrical slow movement, and a bubbling rondo. In the first movement he continues the aforementioned practice of alternating chromatic and diatonic passages. The Tema is a twenty-four bar tripartite structure in which the middle section contains two brief bars of chromatic movement in the piano that function as a seed from which the highly chromatic second variation grows. It is surrounded by the primarily diatonic first and third variations. The second movement is a beautifully sustained lyrical statement that is built both melodically and harmonically on the C/F# bichord that opens the movement. The final movement alternates two contrasting ideas—one athletic in character and the other lyric.

The trumpet and piano are equal partners in this work as the thematic material in all three movements alternates between the two in a concerted fashion. While there is ample opportunity for technical display in the third movement, this sonata is much more than a vehicle for the display of virtuosity. It is basically a sincere, at times almost reverent work that requires extreme sensitivity on the part of both performers. It is also another example of the artistic quality that results when skill and craftsmanship combine with creative imagination.

6

Keyboard Music

For a composer who is an accomplished performer on both piano and organ, Dello Joio has written a surprisingly small amount of music for solo keyboard. The list of works for keyboard instruments includes twenty-three compositions for piano, one for harpsichord or piano, and three for organ. (This list does not include the compositions for piano and orchestra that were discussed in chapter 4.) Among these works are extended compositions such as the three piano sonatas, short character pieces such as the two nocturnes, and pedagogic music, some of which was written for the musical development of Dello Joio's three children. All but two of these works have been published. A *Rhumba* and *Duo Concertante*, both for two pianos, exist in manuscript form only.

The earliest keyboard work to be published is the Suite for piano, a group of four contrasting pieces for piano solo that was composed in the spring of 1940. The original title was *Sandburg Phrases*, and the work was premiered under that title on 9 March 1941 by Lillian Lefkovsky at Carnegie Chamber Music Hall. The pieces are contrasting sketches in free moods suggested by the following lines from Carl Sandburg:

1 "Out of the window . . . prairie lands."
2 "Why does a hearse horse sniker hauling a lawyer away?"
3 "The whistle of a boat calls and cries unendingly."
4 "The cartoonists weep in their beer."

Frequent metrical changes and emphasis on the interval of a fourth are characteristic of all the pieces. The perfect fourth is featured often as a melodic interval, and the harmonic language contains a mixture of quartal and tertian structures. All of the pieces are firmly grounded in tonality. The respective tonal centers are E-flat, B-flat, F-sharp, and B-flat.

The first piece in Suite for piano moves at a moderate pace and is constructed in two sections which begin respectively in bars 1 and 12. The second section is a varied repetition of the first. The second piece moves at a brisk pace with the use of irregular, off-beat accents to give added rhythmic interest to the simple meters of 3/4 and 4/4. Melodic interest is provided by the use of an ostinato pattern in the lydian mode that is played against the principal melody in the mixolydian mode. The third piece is calm and nocturnal. A choralelike melody in half notes in an inner voice moves in contrary motion to the melody in the bass while the eighth note figures in the treble provide atmosphere. The final piece is ferocious, featuring driving, triplet rhythms, and exploiting the percussive capabilities of the piano. A two-bar motive first heard in bars 22–23 is the principal melodic element, but the sixteenth note figure in bar 1 also figures prominently near the end of the piece. While the pieces in this suite reveal a kind of youthful exuberance and freshness of invention, they also exhibit the economical use of material and craftsmanship that are characteristic of the composer's more mature works.

The circumstances surrounding the composition of Dello Joio's first piano sonata are interesting and somewhat amusing. On a day near the end of January 1943, Dello Joio was caught in a sudden downpour on the streets of New York. He ducked inside a doorway where concert pianist Sidney Foster just happened to be standing to await the end of the deluge. The two engaged in conversation. Foster said, "I'm playing a recital in Carnegie Hall in two weeks. Why don't you write something for me?" Dello Joio replied, "Well it's kind of short notice, but sure, I'll do it."[1] So, between 1 and 4 February 1943 Dello Joio composed the first of his three piano sonatas. Foster learned it in a week, and played it from memory at his recital.

Although the sonata is cast in the traditional three-movement form of the classical sonata, the individual movements are inspired by musical forms of the baroque period. The respective titles are "Chorale Prelude," "Canon," and "Capriccio." The monothematic first movement is based on a choralelike melody in the dorian mode that borrows some notes from the key of G-flat. The melody is first heard as a monodic line over a tonic pedal. On repetition it is reinforced at the octave. It is then submitted to a series of modifications that include transposition, rhythmic augmentation, and fragmentation. After reaching its climax in bar 82, the movement subsides into a quiet close as the melody is stated once again, but in augmented form. Three repetitions of the D-major triad bring the movement to its end.

The calm second movement is a canon at the octave based on a phrygian melody with A as its tonal center. Following two repetitions of the minor third B-flat–G in the low register, the canon begins in bar 3 in the top voice of the right hand. The imitation must be listened for carefully as it is sounded in the tenor voice of a dissonant, four-part contrapuntal texture. After the intricacies of the canonical structure have been worked through, the movement closes with repetitions of the opening minor third under an increasingly dissonant progression of chords that rise to a climax and then resolve to a G-minor seventh chord.

The "Capriccio" moves forward with driving syncopated rhythmic figures and frequent metrical shifts. Set in ABA′ form, it begins with a twelve-bar introduction utilizing massive tertian chords of the ninth, eleventh, and thirteenth. The principal theme (bar 13) is a six-bar melody of classical proportions and tonality. Set in A major, the first half outlines the tonic triad and progresses to the dominant note E. The second half begins on E and returns to tonic. The harmony is not conventional, however, as dissonant seconds and sevenths abound. The B section (bar 78) is a brief, cantabile interlude between the more vigorous outer sections. Of ornamental interest here is the use of grace notes a ninth below the principal notes of the melody. The return of the principal theme is first heard in the bass register, and subsequently returns to the treble. As is the case with most of Dello Joio's ternary structures, the final section is abbreviated.

Of the three piano sonatas that Dello Joio composed, the second, which was composed 2–29 September 1943 is most closely related to the classical sonata in design and formal structure. The three movements are Presto martellato, Adagio, and Vivace spiritoso.

The first movement presents two contrasting ideas—the first, driving and percussive, and the second, cantabile. Each is developed immediately after its initial presentation. Following the development of the second idea, the essential elements of the first idea return to give the movement a ternary form. The tonal center of C is firmly established at the opening by reiteration of the note C with octave doublings in strong rhythmic positions through the first twenty bars. This tonal center is reaffirmed in the last three bars with the sounding of the C natural minor scale and a strong cadence to a C chord with missing 3d. In between, a very free use of the twelve tones in the octave results in frequent shifts of mode. The meter is 3/4 throughout, but the persistent use of two dotted quarters against three quarters results in a polymetric feeling of 3/4 against 6/8. Of harmonic interest is the frequent use of the dyad rather than the triad as the basis of harmonic structure. In bars 7–9, a passage begins at the unison and moves two lines in contrary motion through the notes of the diatonic scale so that the resulting succession of intervals is unison, third, fifth, seventh, ninth—a simple but effective tension building device. In bars 41–43, chromatic rather than diatonic movement results in the inclusion of the fourth and sixth in the succession of intervals. The entire movement is an interesting intervallic study in so much as the harmonic movement is created without relying on traditional harmonic schemes, but on the color and tension-producing characteristics of the intervals possible within the twelve note scale. Although examples of functional harmony can be found elsewhere in Dello Joio's music, in this particular movement it is totally absent.

The Adagio is a highly chromatic movement that makes effective use of ostinati in the bass. Melody is not an important element. This is an evocative movement that depends on sonority and ornamental keyboard figures for effect. There are prominent motives, but nothing that could be called a tune. The tonality is A-flat minor with a modulation to E minor for the middle section of the three part form. However, because of the extensive chromatic movement, a definite key feeling is lacking much of the time. The pianist with small hands should beware. A reach of an eleventh is required in the left hand, and the notation indicates that the two notes should be played together, not one slightly ahead of the other.

The third movement is in rondo form with the themes presented in a contrapuntal texture that ranges from three to four voices. The order in which the material is presented is as follows: A (bars 1–30); B (bars 31–57); C (bars 58–76); A/B (bars 77–90); B (bars 91–106); A (bars 107–21). The A theme is an expansive F-sharp aeolian melody performed cantabile over an ostinato pattern in the left hand. The B theme is a two-bar motive that was derived by inverting and augmenting the left hand accompanying figure in bar 12. It is presented in both treble and bass registers in original and inverted form. The third idea is another expansive, cantabile melody stated once in the treble register and then in modified form in the bass register. It should be noted that Dello Joio seldom repeats a theme exactly as it was stated originally. Repetition of the theme is almost always varied in some way. The variation may be slight, as bars 87–89 where the A theme is simply transposed up a fourth and abbreviated, or it may be extreme, as in bars 107–20 where only the remnants of the accompanying figure of A are heard as the piece draws to a close.

Dello Joio's bent toward lyricism is evident in the *Prelude to a Young Musician* (1943). Composed in ABA' form, the piece features a beautiful E-major melody in a consonant setting in the A section while the progression of harmonies is the most interesting element in the B section. The transition to the A' section is noteworthy. At the close of the middle section a portion of the A theme is heard in the bass register in the key of F-flat (enharmonic E) thus effecting an enharmonic modulation back to E, but the A theme returns in B major and remains in that key until the final close to an E^7 chord.

Lyricism is also present in *Prelude to a Young Dancer* (1943), but the C-sharp aeolian melody is presented in a dissonant contrapuntal texture. Both this piece and *Young Musician* show irregular groupings of rhythmic figures that counter the regular pulse as in this example:
6/8 ♪ ♫ ♫ ♪♫ ♫ ♫ ♪

During the year 1945, Dello Joio made two arrangements of the music from his ballet *On Stage*, one for piano solo and one for piano duet. In 1946, he wrote the Nocturne in F-sharp which was published in 1950 along with the Nocturne in E that he composed in that year. Although composed four years apart, both nocturnes are charming twentieth-century adaptations of Chopin's idiom. There is something of a neo-Chopinesque flow in the Nocturne in E, though with some dissonant touches that would have been highly suspect in 1835. The Nocturne in F-sharp contains echoes of Gershwin with its use of "blue notes" from the jazz idiom.

Dello Joio's best known composition for the piano is probably Sonata no. 3.[2] Composed in May 1947 it is based on the same thematic material—the "Kyrie" from the *Mass of Angels*—as *Variations, Chaconne, and Finale*, which was started one month earlier, yet neither work is an arrangement of the other.[3] The orchestral work is cast in three movements, the sonata in four. The greatest similarities exist between the first and last movements of the respective works. Both first movements consist of a set of variations based on the "Kyrie" theme (see example 10). The orchestral work has six variations with coda, and the piano sonata has five variations with practically the same coda. Further brief comparisons are: piano variation 1 is derived from orchestra variation 3; piano variation 2 compares with orchestra variation 5; piano variation 3 comes from orchestra variation 4, bars 145–50 and 165–70; piano vari-

ation 4 was orchestra variation 1; and piano variation 5 is similar in introduction, variation, and treatment to orchestra variation 6. Movement 2
of the piano sonata is similar in character to the orchestral "Finale," but
the two have no common thematic material. The same may be said of
the third movement of the piano sonata and the orchestral *Chaconne.* It
is between the last movements of the respective works that striking
similarities again occur. The same thematic material is used in both. Despite these similarities, the two compositions are true to their respective
media. The orchestral piece is a large work, brilliantly orchestrated and
highly colorful; the piano sonata is a distillation of the larger work that is
much less heroic in character.

The basic character of the set of variations which comprise the first
movement of Sonata no. 3 has been discussed in connection with *Variations, Chaconne, and Finale* in chapter 3, and need not be repeated here.
Movement 2 is a complete contrast in style and mood to the first movement. It springs from jazz with its use of syncopation, boogie bass pattern, and rumba rhythm. Harmony and melody play minimal roles as the
rhythm is preeminent with its emphasis on cross accents, asymmetrical
division, and implied polymeter. Note in example 22 how the three-beat
boogie pattern in the bass extends across the bar line creating cross
accents with the syncopated two-beat rhythm in the lower voice of the
right hand. The implied meter in the left hand is 3/4 + 3/4 + 2/4.

Example 22. Sonata no. 3 for piano, 2, bars 40–43

The form is ABCA'. The A section treats a syncopated two-bar motive that recurs almost continuously, undergoing changes of accompaniment and tonality. The motive, built of three different tones within the range of a fourth, is mostly played between two tones a major second apart. The key center is defined in bar 5 with the cadence to D-flat major. Section B in E major subsists to an even greater degree on the two-note figure that was so prominent in A. Toward the end of this section the two-note figure of a major second evolves to a minor third (C#–A#) that anticipates enharmonically the D-flat–B-flat figure that is to begin section C. Polytonality is suggested in part C. Using principally black key pentatonic notes, the tonality in the right hand leans toward B-flat minor, and the left hand toward E-flat minor. The passage culminates in two bars of $3/8 + 3/8 + 2/8$ rumba rhythm. This rhythm continues after the key change to E major, and the climax of the movement is reached with the use of repeated triads in the treble against a dissonant bass. Motivic figures in the bass lead to a low D-flat which completes the climax and signals the beginning of the final section in which motivic dissolution leads to a quiet close.

The third movement is a quiet, contemplative interlude that is cast in ABA' form. Part A begins in low register with its principle theme in the upper voice—a well ornamented cantabile melody that begins in the lydian mode. Part B is passive and impressionistic in effect. Its main theme is presented twice—once in E-flat minor and once in B-flat minor. The texture consists of a legato melody and three very soft accompanying voices with bell-like fifths in the highest voice, melodic minor thirds in the voice underneath, and the bass frequently alternating between tonic and dominant. Following the second statement of the B theme, a transition to A' anticipates the return with the melodic figures centering around A-flat in bar 35. The shortened reprise contains only one statement of the theme.

The fourth movement is a fast, playful movement in cut time. It is full of ostinati, shifted and cross accents, asymmetrical division, crossing of hands, and virtual polymeter. It begins and ends in E major and is diatonic for long stretches. Even though rhythmic motion is of paramount interest, melodic lyricism is also present in this movement. The principal theme in the ABA' form consists of two three-bar phrases (example 23). In the first phrase a descending scale is heard against a repeated pitch in the upper voice. The second phrase is more distinctive as the upper voice ascends the octave E–E, and then descends scalewise to B, after which the lower voice answers by ascending a seventh from B to A and

Example 23. Sonata no. 3 for piano, 4, bars 10–15

returns scalewise to tonic. Following the development of this theme, the transition to the second theme begins with modified portions of material from movement 2.

The second theme of movement 4 begins as an expansive melody in middle register. It proceeds at a leisurely pace accompanied by triadic harmonies with an added ninth placed in the bass line. To bring this section to a climax the composer departs from tonic, begins a lengthy crescendo with ascending pitch level, thickens the texture, and uses chromatic harmony over an E-flat pedal. The climax smashes its way into a bar of rest (bar 95). Following that, an eleven bar retransition derived from the introduction leads to the final section.

The final section recapitulates the theme in modified form as it undergoes rhythmic augmentation and melodic alteration. Solidly in the key of E, the dominant is emphasized until near the end. Beginning in bar 134, a thematic motive begins monodically and is joined by an additional voice every bar for five bars. This rapid increase in textural density combines with the continuous rumba rhythm and pandiatonic harmony (using all seven scale tones) to build a tremendous climax prior to the final cadence in which tonic and dominant are sounded together before the final resolution to a perfect fifth dyad on E.

With the *Aria and Toccata* for two pianos (1952), Dello Joio once again put to use the formal molds of the baroque era. The addition of a second piano allowed him to use massive organlike sonorities, multivoice contrapuntal texture, and occasional antiphonal effects. A monothematic aria in three sections of contrasting tempi precedes a spirited toccata in which shifting accents and syncopation again make the rhythm one of the more notable elements.

Following the completion of the *Aria and Toccata*, Dello Joio did not write for solo keyboard again until 1962. During that time he was occupied with the composition of three operas, and a number of commissioned works for television and film. *The Ballad of the Seven Lively Arts* and *Fantasy and Variations*, both for piano and orchestra, also date from this period.

During the last two decades Dello Joio has devoted considerable time to writing music for the young pianist. Motivated by the musical development of his children, he wrote *Family Album* (1962) and *Five Images* (1966) expressly for them. Both sets are for one piano (four hands). *Family Album* contains five charming pieces written in a simple style that a beginning pianist could easily grasp. *Five Images* is a more demanding set as it reflects his children's musical development over a four year period.

Suite for the Young (1964) is a collection of ten short pieces for piano solo. Technically they are easy, but there is ample musical interest. They are excellent pieces with which the young musician may be introduced to some aspects of twentieth century harmonic and melodic practices. "Mountain Melody" for example is a short piece of twenty-two bars with a simple C-major melody accompanied by added-note chords that sometimes create dissonant clashes such as C-sharp against C natural in bar 5. "Invention" contains triadic melodies in both hands—major triads in the right hand and minor triads in the left hand. The triads have a major/ relative minor relationship when sounded in succession. Together they form a minor-major seventh chord. The last piece is a lesson in text setting that requires the performer to write or sing the words of the "Lord's Prayer" according to the "Choral Chant" that the composer has written.

Other compositions that Dello Joio has written with the young pianist in mind include *Lyric Pieces for the Young* (1971), *Diversions* (1975), both for piano solo, and *Stage Parodies* (1974) for piano duet. Piano pedagogs who are looking for worthy contemporary literature of easy to moderate difficulty would do well to investigate these pieces.

Night Song (1963) represents Dello Joio's first excursion into twelve tone writing. It is a short character piece that utilizes widely spaced, sustained pitches and arpeggios to create an effective mood. Tritonal relationships also play a significant role. The piece is based on four triads (DFA, CEG, F#A#C#, G#B#D#) which have tritonal root relationships and form a twelve tone row when sounded in succession.

Capriccio on the Interval of a Second (1968) was commissioned for the Third Van Cliburn Quadrennial International Piano Competition at Fort Worth, Texas, as the required contemporary composition for all contestants. The work opens with a slow introduction that returns in abbreviated form at the end. The main body of the piece is fast and vigorous. As the title suggests, the melodic movement in the introduction is primarily stepwise. Tertian structures dominate the harmony, but with the notes arranged so that the interval of a second is always present somewhere in the chord. A brief cantibile section begins at bar 15 which features running parallel thirds in the right hand over an ostinato pattern of major and minor seconds in the left hand. Reinforcement of the top pitch at the octave leads to the climax of this section in which the triple octave descending second B–A is sounded repeatedly in double dotted rhythm. The texture is thickened with each repetition to increase the tension even further. Following this tremendous burst of energy, the texture is thinned and the music tapers into the Allegro section.

The composer might have chosen the title "rondo capriccioso" for this loud and boistrous Allegro. The formal plan is A (bars 25–39), B (bars 40–58), C (bars 59–71), D (bars 73–83), B' (bars 84–87), A' (bars 88–91), C' (bars 92–100); B" (bars 101–14), A" (bars 115–21), B''' (bars 122–38). Lyricism does not play a significant role here. The interest is provided by the energetic, accentuated rhythms, textural and harmonic contrasts. Dissonant clashes and cross relationships are plentiful, and brief polytonal passages may be observed in bars 51–52 and 84–85. Agitation is achieved by such techniques as changing suddenly from a progression of large tertian chords performed marcatissimo to a single monophonic line (bars 43 and 61), or interrupting a crescendo with an unexpected rest (bars 59 and 72). The whole is unified by rhythmic variations on the interval of a second. Note in example 24 how the shifting rhythmic accents in the left hand maintain interest while the melody and harmony remain relatively static. In example 25 the pitch relationships are the same, but the rhythm is even and the notes are slurred. This kind of extreme variation in types of articulation requires superb control by the performer, undoubtedly a conscious choice by the composer for a piece designed to test the abilities of some of the world's finest young pianists.

Example 24. *Capriccio,* bars 28–30

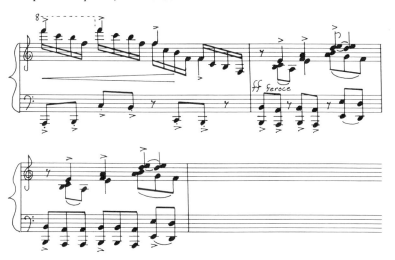

Example 25. *Capriccio,* bars 75–78

Dello Joio's two most recent compositions for piano are a set of four sonatas for piano or harpsichord collectively titled *Salute to Scarlatti* (1979), and a set of *Concert Variations for Piano* (1980). Just as the *Two Nocturnes* mentioned earlier are an effective modern adaptation of Chopin's idiom, the four sonatas are a faithful twentieth century representation of the Baroque master of the keyboard, Domenico Scarlatti (1685–1757). The *Concert Variations* are another indication of Dello Joio's abiding interest in the variations form and his skillful mastery of the technique of development from an extremely small fragment of thematic material.

It seems ironic that a composer who descended from three generations of Italian organists and was trained as an organist himself did not write a composition for the organ until he was fifty-two years old. The reason resides partly in the fact that the organ is so closely associated with liturgical music, and having once rejected the opportunity to become a career church musician, Dello Joio spent his creative energy establishing himself as a composer in the secular concert world. It was not until the summer of 1965, when he received two commissions for organ compositions, that Dello Joio wrote for that instrument. A commission from Nita Akin and the Aeolian Skinner Organ Company for the dedication of the new recital organ at Southern Methodist University resulted in *Laudation*, a one movement work for organ solo. A second commission from Austin Organs led to the composition of *Antiphonal Fantasy* for organ, brass, and strings.

Laudation is a colorful work designed to exploit the massive sonorities of the Aeolian Skinner organ. The structure of the music is based on the principle of organic growth that is so characteristic of Dello Joio's writing during this period. (See the discussion of *Songs of Walt Whitman* in chapter 2 and *Fantasy and Variations* in chapter 4.) Following an overall plan of ABA', the work begins with an introduction that announces a three note motive (example 26) from which the material in the A section germinates.

Example 26. *Laudation,* bars 1–4

The introduction consists of a series of six four-bar phrases followed by a five bar transition leading to the A theme. The germinal motive contains a descending major second followed by a descending perfect fourth. In the first phrase the motive is stated and answered immediately by its inversion. The chord that follows contains all of the pitches heard in the preceding succession of notes. The second phrase is a repetition of the first phrase an octave higher followed by a rhythmic augmentation of the motive in the pedals. In the third phrase the motivic contour is enlarged through intervalic expansion as the major second becomes a minor third and the perfect fourth an augmented fifth in the right hand, and the respective intervals in the inversion are major third and perfect fifth. Again the fourth phrase is an octave transposition of the third. The rhythm begins to gain momentum in the fifth and sixth phrases which are constructed by using the intervalic relationships of the previous phrases. This is followed by a five bar transition of parallel tertian chords in pandiatonic harmony that leads to the A theme (example 27).

The A theme consists of two four-bar phrases. The first begins with two repetitions of the original three-note motive of the introduction. The second is also derived from this motive, but in a less obvious manner. The descending second can be observed in action in bar 36. Examination of the remainder of the A section will reveal the presence of motivically derived material in practically every bar. Also to be noted in example 27 is the use of bichordal harmony which tends to obscure the tonality. The progression in bars 30–31 is A/C B/Ab C/Gb D/F C/Gb B/Ab A + 2. With the use of harmonic structures such as these, the repeated C's in the pedals are needed to establish C as the tonal center.

Example 27. *Laudation,* bars 30–39

The slow, expressive B section provides effective contrast to the energetic outer sections. It closes with a quotation of the germinal motive in inverted form. With the return to fast tempo, the motive is expanded into what sounds like the beginning of a fugue. As it turns out however, it is only a monophonic transition back to the A theme which is recapitulated in customary abbreviated form.

The *Antiphonal Fantasy* is built on a theme by the seventeenth century Italian composer Vincenzo Albrici (1631–96).[4] The work is dedicated to Dello Joio's former teacher Paul Hindemith, who died in 1963. The world premiere of *Antiphonal Fantasy* was originally scheduled for the four concerts opening the 1966–67 season of the Philadephia Orchestra with Eugene Ormandy conducting and Richard Ellsasser as soloist. Because the musician's union called a strike against that orchestra, the concerts were postponed, and the work did not receive its first performance in Philadelphia until the opening of the 1967–68 season. The world premiere took place in Tulsa, Oklahoma, on 12 December 1966 with Franco Autori conducting the Tulsa Philharmonic and Ellsasser as soloist. The work was also performed by the Houston, Pittsburgh, Detroit, and Cincinnati Symphony orchestras. Following the premiere performance, the Tulsa Daily World called *Antiphonal Fantasy* ". . . a tremendous work combining varied elements into a thoroughly harmonious whole and ending on a jubilant note," and stated further that "No new work ever played by the Tulsa Philharmonic Orchestra has been so warmly received."

Writing for the *Philadelphia Orchestra Program Book*, Dello Joio stated:

The *Antiphonal Fantasy* is scored for solo organ, a full compliment of brass and strings. The constant play in imitation between organ, brass and strings dictated the title of the work. Despite the fact that I was an organist during the first half of my career, it is the first symphonic work I have written for organ.

The form of the work can be loosely described as a three-part form, after a lengthy introduction that indicates the thematic material. The manipulation of the three distinct groups has its roots in the antiphonal music of the early Italian church composers, particularly the Gabrielis.[5]

From the composer's own description, it is plain that the form of *Antiphonal Fantasy* is very similar to *Laudation*. In the slow introduction tritonal relationships are used to maintain suspense, and dissonant chords are used to build tension towards the opening statement of the Albrici

Example 28. *Antiphonal Fantasy,* bars 35–37

theme (example 28) which is given in C major and harmonized in early baroque style. There follows a development section that utilizes thematic material, but returns to a contemporary harmonic language.

The calm slow section, which features a contrasting lyrical theme, is followed by a reworking of the material from the introduction which in turn leads to the final section in which both themes are restated to bring the work to a brilliant close.

The instrumentation is calculated to achieve splendid, colorful effects, particularly from brass and organ. The overall result is a powerful work that effectively blends early and modern styles.

Dello Joio's only other work for organ is the set of *Five Lyric Pieces for the Young Organist* (1975). These pieces are simply organ transcriptions of the five pieces for piano called *Diversions.* The set contains a Preludio, an Arietta, a Caccia, a Chorale, and a Giga. The last two are based on the tune *"In dulci jubilo"* which is the subject for variation in two of Dello Joio's compositions for band (see chapter 7).

Although Dello Joio's keyboard works represent a small percentage of his total output, the study of them will prove rewarding because they reveal the essential elements of his style, and they represent excellent writing by a composer who, by virtue of his extensive training as a pianist and organist, thoroughly understands the performing medium. Having decided early in his career to become a composer, Dello Joio did not devote a great deal of time to concertizing. Nevertheless, the fact that he has appeared as an executant of his own works with organizations such as the New York Philharmonic under George Szell, is evidence of his skill and accomplishment as a performer.

Looking back on the list of keyboard works, it may be observed that the bulk of Dello Joio's creative output for this medium occurred during the early years of his career. With the exception of those works that fall in the category of pedagogic music, the *Capriccio*, and the compositions for organ, all of the keyboard works were composed between 1940 and 1952. Since that time his primary attention has been devoted to composition for other media. Whether or not the *Salute to Scarlatti* and *Concert Variations* represent the beginning of a renewed interest in writing for keyboard remains to be seen.

7

Music for Band

Dello Joio's first composition for band dates from the year 1963 when he had already reached maturity, and had received critical acclaim as one of America's outstanding composers. His orchestral works had been performed and recorded by the major orchestras both in this country and abroad. His chamber works were eagerly sought out by the leading performing artists of this era, and his choral works were among those American works most frequently performed. In short, he had already made his mark on the American musical scene, and that mark would remain even if he never wrote a note for band. Why should he have turned to a new performing medium at this point in his career? There are several reasons. First, Dello Joio is a composer who wants his music to be performed and heard by a broad cross section of the public, not just those who regularly attend classical music concerts. However, the opportunity to hear a live performance of an orchestral work by an American composer has always been a rarity. That fact coupled with the trend toward the international avant-garde style among those in professional circles (a trend that Dello Joio steadfastly refused to follow) meant that the orchestral scene held little promise for him. *Blood Moon*, his first full length opera, premiered in 1961, but because of the negative reviews by a few key critics, the prospects of getting additional performances of that work or a new opera were at best discouraging. Second, Dello Joio loves young people. He enjoys being with them socially and working with them in an educational setting. His involvement with the Young Composers Project and CMP brought him into direct contact with this country's public school and college music programs, and he became aware that an abundance of musical talent existed in the performing organizations of educational institutions in this country and that bands far outnumbered orchestras. Because the concert band lacked the vast amount of repertoire that had been developed for orchestras over the past three centuries, modern composers were being called upon to fill this void. The opportunity to write for band therefore offered Dello Joio a new and promising creative outlet. Upon receipt of a commission from the Mary Duke Biddle Foundation to write a work for the Duke University Band, he made it a point to get to know the band. He studied and mastered problems of range, dynamics, balance, and articulation among the various instruments that comprise the wind ensemble. His scoring for band is creative and resourceful, making full use of every section of the ensemble. His knowledge of the expressive resources of the band is particularly apparent in the slow movements. Here he has managed to create an intensity of emotional expression that few composers in this medium have been able to achieve. The fast movements reveal the same kind of unrestrained exuberance that is evident in his orchestral works.

Dello Joio's first composition for band is *Variants on a Medieval Tune* which was premiered on 10 April 1963. The tune in question is the familiar "In dulci jubilo," a melody that has been used by many composers as the subject for a variety of musical settings. Dello Joio used as his model the chorale setting by J. S. Bach.[1] Employing the variations procedures that he had found so satisfying in his orchestral works, he commenced exploring the inherent possibilities of "In dulci jubilo." He found them to be abundant, for he did not stop with the five variations heard in this work. One movement of *Scenes from the Louvre* (1965) and all thirteen movements of *Colonial Variants* (1976), of which six were extracted and scored for band under the title *Colonial Ballads*, are based on this same tune. The tune has a striking resemblance to the "Kyrie" theme that was the subject of *Variations, Chaconne, and Finale* (the first six scale tones of both melodies are identical), a fact that has prompted some critics to accuse Dello Joio of being repetitive in his work. To the casual observer who listens only for the tune, that may appear to be so. However, for the more attentive it will become apparent that for Dello Joio the tune is not the end, but the means which stimulates the composer's creative imagination and tests his skill. Among the twenty variations on "In dulci jubilo" that he composed, there is only one instance of repetition. Movements 6 and 7 of *Colonial Variants* are a reworking of Movement 3 of *Variants on a Medieval Tune*. Each of the other variations examines the tune in a new light and demonstrate once again the composer's skill at discovering the myriad possibilities for variation that are present in even the simplest diatonic melody.

Dello Joio also employed the variations principle in *Fantasies on a Theme by Haydn* (1968).[2] The first eight bars of Haydn's theme are quoted in example 29. They should be examined closely because Dello Joio derives all of his material from the theme itself. There is very little free fantasy. Practically every note in the score can be related to the theme in one way or another.

Example 29. F. J. Haydn, String Quartet, op. 76, no. 2, movement 4, violin 1, bars 1–8

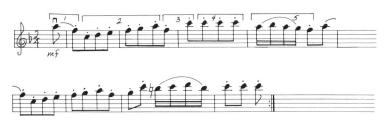

Even though the theme is thirty-four bars in length, its essential elements are contained in the first four bars. Those four bars contain five melodic events (indicated with brackets in the example) that Dello Joio uses to create his "Fantasies." They are as follows: 1) the descending third beginning on an eighth note pick-up; 2) the ascending scale figure from C to A; 3) the upward leap of a fifth from F to C; 4) the repetition of the pitch C on four successive eighth notes; 5) the sixteenth note turn around the pitch A.

The frolicking first movement begins with a thirty-eight bar introduction that is followed by the statement of the theme and a short coda. To build his introduction Dello Joio took the thematic fragments listed above and manipulated them by means of chromatic alteration, change of mode, and dissonant harmony so that they only hint at what is to come. With a couple of minor exceptions, the entire theme is then stated just as Haydn wrote it, but with the accompanying parts written by Dello Joio.

Fantasy I continues the same tempo and mood as the Introduction, but with the meter changed to 4/4. It is cast in three sections, each of which examine the theme in a different light. The first section (bars 105–23) opens with an ostinato pattern played by bass clarinet, bassoon, and bari-

tone horn that is derived from the theme. The first four notes (A B*b* A
G) are a rhythmic augmentation of event 5, and the next three notes (A
E*b* C) are a melodic diminution of events 3 and 1. This figure serves as
a lead-in to the statement of the theme by the trombones in bar 114—a
rhythmically altered statement in the lydian mode. Although space does
not permit a detailed account of every bar in the score, a close scrutiniz-
ation of bars 110–15 will illustrate how not only the trombone part, but
every note on the page is thematically derived. The descending thirds
played by flutes, second clarinets, and glockenspiel are simply an extension of event 1. The descending scale passages played by piccolo, oboe,
and third clarinets amount to the same thing with the thirds filled in with
passing notes. The cornets in bars 111–12 play a disguised entry that
begins with notes three through nine of the theme. Take the ostinatolike
figure played by the tubas, third and fourth trombones, bassoons, and
bass clarinet in bars 111–12, omit the B natural, and what remains are
the first five notes of the theme in order. Finally, the ascending scale
played by trumpets and French horns in bars 114–15 is a rhythmic augmentation of event 2. The fact that all these events work well together
attests to Dello Joio's skill as a contrapuntist and the economy of means
that he is able to use in developing a complex passage of music.

The second section of Fantasy I (bars 125–45) offers two variants of
the theme. Both use tonal materials from two different modes simultaneously. The first (bar 126), played by first clarinets with reinforcement
from tenor saxophones and bass clarinet, mixes the A-flat major and F
minor modes. The second (bar 133), played by baritone horn and all
woodwinds except bassoon, emphasizes the tritonal relationship of the
D-flat and G-major scales. The remainder of this section is an extension
of the second variant by means of rhythmic dimunition and thematic fragmentation. The third section (bars 146–79) presents rhythmically modified statements of the theme in D-flat major and C-major before the
movement builds to a climax with a succession of motivic figures based
on events 1 and 2.

Fantasy 2 is a slow, intensely lyrical movement that provides contrast
to the bubbling humor of the movements that flank it. The opening statement of the theme omits the falling third. It is on the F-major scale, but
harmonized with dissonant seconds and sevenths whose need to move
toward resolution maintains forward motion through the slowly plodding
rhythm. The resolution is achieved with the move to an A-flat major
chord as the tenth note of the theme is reached. Two other more or less
complete statements are heard—one in C-sharp minor (bar 189) and one

in G-flat major (bar 209). The rest of the movement consists of a chain of thematic fragments that move with great fluidity from one tonal area to another until the final close on A major.

The pitch A then becomes the pick-up note for Fantasy 3 as it leaps up to C, and then is answered by a descending third from E-flat to C. The implications of the third and the stepwise ascent of the theme (events 1 and 2) are then carried to great length. The material is reduced to its most basic elements as extremely short fragments of the theme are skillfully combined to construct this movement. Several tonal areas are once again explored with incomplete variants before a final statement in the tonic key is sounded (bar 362). A brief coda then brings the work to a rousing climax. The music is a fitting tribute to the older master. It does a masterful job of capturing the wit and good humor of the bubbling Haydn rondo that inspired it.

Concertante for Wind Instruments (1972) was commissioned by the North Hills High School Symphony Band, Pittsburgh, Pennsylvania. The work is in two contrasting movements, Adagio molto sostenuto, and Allegro con brio.

The first movement opens with a melodic twelve tone statement (example 30) that indicates thematic material that binds the total composition. Two characteristics of the row should be noted because of the implications they have for the work as a whole. First, the first and last notes (G and C) have a dominant-tonic relationship that defines the tonality of the work—C major. Second, the half step is the most common interval. There are four half steps in the row. The row divides into three groups of four notes each, each of which begins with a half step. It will be noted that all subsequent nonthematic material contains extensive chromatic movement. A third factor that should be mentioned is the way in which the composer achieves melodic continuity in the construction of the row itself. Each of the three groups of four notes has certain characteristics that relate to the previous group. The half step relationship has already been mentioned. In addition, the second group is a modified inversion of the first group, and the third group, except for the last interval, is an exact imitation of the second.

Example 30. *Concertante for Wind Instruments,* twelve-tone row from bars 1–7

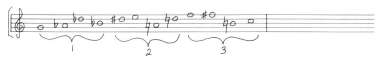

The first movement contains five complete statements of the row that follow the ternary structure outlined below (O = original order; R = retrograde; Int. = interlude):

	A			B	A′			Coda
bar:	1–7	8–12	13–21	22–39	40–45	46–58	59–62	63–73
row:	O	Int.	R	Episode	O	Int.	R.	

Dello Joio described the second movement as a "kaleidoscopic antiphonal dance in 6/8 suggesting a saltarello."[3] It is a sectional form in which the various themes are derived from the tone row of the first movement. The melodic figures quoted in example 31 illustrate the manner in which the composer derives his material from the row.

Example 31. *Concertante for Wind Instruments,* thematically derived motives
            from movement 2

a. bars 13–16
   saxophones

b. bars 17–18
   horns

c. bars 21–22
   trumpets

d. bars 161–63
   piccolo

e. bars 180–84
   trumpets

f. bars 189–92
   piccolo

All of the motives are derived from the first four notes of the row. Motives *a*, *b*, and *c* represent an expansion of the intervals in the original. In *a* and *b* the minor second is expanded to a minor third, and the perfect fourth becomes a perfect fifth. The second bar of *c* carries this even further as the third is expanded to a fourth and the fifth to a sixth. Example 31*d* is simply an octave transposition with the intervals remaining intact. Example 31*e* is derived by contracting the intervals of the original. Notes 2–5 of this motive represent notes 1–4 of the row with the fourth reduced to a third, and the third to a second. The first two bars of example 31*f* are a retrograde version of notes two through five of example 31*e*. With the composer's extremely economical use of his material, the main focus in this movement is on the chain of events that spring from the linear expansion of motivic ideas. The propulsive rhythm and antiphonal use of the different sections of the ensemble heighten the interest while harmonic considerations are of secondary importance. This score is one more example of Dello Joio's tendency to build his composition by starting with a very simple idea, the significance of which cannot be fully comprehended until the listener has explored the entire work.

Dello Joio's other compositions for band are all based on works written originally for other media. In 1963, he received a commission from the New York Port Authority to compose the music for the film *From Every Horizon* that was being made to promote the city of New York and the 1964 World Fair. The film score was completed on 7 March 1964. Upon receipt of a commission from the University of North Dakota for a band composition, Dello Joio took several cues from this film score, reworked them and transcribed them for band. He retained the film title and added the parenthetical expression "A Tone Poem to New York." The band score "recreates a series of moods that are an evocation of the spirit of New York. For example the opening movement reflects the little known pastoral mood that pervades the outskirts of the big town. The hurly-burly of the commuter, the bustle of the typical New Yorker, the tired out-of towner, all inspired the composer in the writing of this score."[4]

The tone poem is written in three movements. The first is in ABA' form and evokes two contrasting moods. The opening section is clearly associated with the pastoral mood mentioned above. A lyrical F-major melody in lilting 6/8 rhythm is accompanied by a progression of tertian chords (sevenths and ninths with occasional added sixths or seconds) the roots of which move primarily by the interval of a second or third. The animated B section in 4/4 meter is more reflective of the "bustle of the typical New Yorker." Piccolo, flutes, and oboes open with an athletic melody that is accompanied by the chatter of sixteenth notes by the clarinets and a brisk walking rhythm in the saxophones and low brass. The French horns enter in bar 35 with a minor variant of the main theme which occurs later in the movement. The sixteenth note chatter continues to build until the trumpets and trombones sound the main theme—a series of parallel triads that move stepwise up and down the F-major scale. A brief excursion to A-flat sets the scene for the return of the A section in abbreviated form.

Movement 2 is a slowly moving Adagio in 4/4 that seems to characterize the "tired out-of-towner." It is lacking in rhythmic energy, and the melodic direction is downward. The effect is aided by the use of the A-minor tonality. Two melodic ideas are heard before the movement draws to a quiet close with a progression to G^7 (V of C) to facilitate the opening of the energetic third movement in C major.

The second and third movements are connected by the sustained G that sounds until the trumpets and trombones enter fortissimo with two bars of tonic ninth that support a joyful C-major theme in the woodwinds. The movement then progresses in the fashion of a spirited rondo. The plan is ABCBCAB + coda. The B theme is a return of the main theme of the animato section of movement 1. By closing with this theme, Dello Joio effectively ties the whole work together.

Scenes from the Louvre was commissioned by Baldwin Wallace College for the Baldwin Wallace Symphonic Band. Dello Joio conducted the premiere on 13 March 1966. The music is taken from the score of the NBC television special "The Louvre" which was composed and transcribed by Dello Joio in 1964 (see chapter 8). *Scenes from the Louvre* then consists of an Introduction which is based on the title music from the film score, followed by a happy collection of baroque tunes all skillfully arranged and brilliantly scored for band. Movement 2, "Children's Gallery," is a transcription of Tielman Susato's "Ronde and Saltarello."[5] Movement 3, "The Kings of France," is based on themes of Jean Baptiste Lully who did noble service as court composer to Louis XIV. Movement 4, "The Nativity Paintings," is yet another variation of "In dulci jubilo." The final movement, "Finale," is based on Albrici's "Festiliche Sonate"[6] (example 28) which Dello Joio used also in the *Antiphonal Fantasy for Organ, Brass, and Strings*.

In 1969, Dello Joio received a commission from Kappa Kappa Psi and Tau Beta Sigma to write a band composition for the fiftieth anniversary celebration of the founding of Kappa Kappa Psi. For this occasion he composed *Songs of Abelard* which was premiered by members of the fraternity and sorority sponsored National Intercollegiate Band on 22 August 1969, with the composer conducting. The music is based on the ballet *Time of Snow*, a dance score that Dello Joio had composed for the Martha Graham Dance Company in 1968. He described *Songs of Abelard* as a "symphonic synthesis culled from the music of *Time of Snow*."[7] The band work is scored for baritone solo (a baritone horn can be substituted in the absence of a vocalist) and complete symphony band.

The introduction and three movements of *Songs of Abelard* are concerned with the dramatic and tragic story of Abelard and Heloise. Peter Abelard (1079–1142) was one of the foremost scholars of his day and father of the University of Paris. He was engaged by Fulbert, the canon of Notre Dame, as a tutor for his seventeen year old niece, Heloise. A love affair between the two invoked the wrath of Fulbert, and the young couple fled to Brittany where she bore him a son. Abelard and Heloise were secretly married and returned to Paris. When Fulbert began to expose them to public ridicule and malice, Abelard sent Heloise to a convent for protection. Fulbert, suspecting Abelard of planning to abandon his niece, sent his thugs to Abelard's residence where they brutally attacked and emasculated him. Heloise became a nun and remained at the convent. Abelard, forsaking all hopes of a canonical life, became a monk, thus prompting the exchange of their famous love letters. When he died, his body was taken secretly to her convent at Paraclete and buried there. Twenty-two years later Heloise was buried beside him. In 1817, the remains of both were reburied in the cemetery of Pere-Lachaise, in Paris, where young lovers to this day bring flowers to their grave.[8]

The Introduction opens with the baritone soloist singing of the two lovers:

Example 32. *Songs of Abelard,* voice line, bars 1–3

His comments are underscored by the ensemble which resolves a dissonant chord to a consonant chord at the end of each phrase. The entire story is summarized in those chords—a tragic life is finally resolved in the serenity of death. The Introduction serves two other important functions. First, the use of the aeolian mode effectively evokes the period of the Middle Ages. Second, the melody of the Introduction determines the melodic material of the three movements that follow. The first two bars often return in the manner of a love motive, and at other points fragments of the baritone melody serve as a starting point for new melodic ideas.

The second movement, a majestic song of praise to the scholar Abelard, is surrounded by two profoundly expressive outer movements that deal with the more tragic elements of the story. Dello Joio's lyric gift is very much at work in this score. The music reveals a composer who obviously was deeply touched by the elements of this story—the courage of young Abelard who dared to become a scholar in an age when the dogmas of the church discouraged independent thought, and the undying faithfullness of the pair of lovers—and was able to couch those feelings in lyrical terms.

Satiric Dances for a Comedy by Aristophanes (1975) resulted from a commission that Dello Joio received from the town of Concord, Massachusetts, to write a work for the Concord Band to premiere during the celebration of its Bicentennial on 19 April 1975. The three movements of this work are based on incidental music that Dello Joio had written for a production of the play *Thezmophoriazousae* (see chapter 8) that was done at Boston University during his tenure as Dean of the School of the Arts. Movement 1 is based on cue 3A, a song that Agathon sings in praise of Leto who makes such beautiful music on the lyre. The second movement is based on cue 7, a tender lyric sung by Euripedes. The final movement is based on the dance music of cue 9. The three movements therefore consist of two short songs and a boisterous dance arranged for concert band.

Dello Joio's two most recent compositions for band are both transcriptions from his own keyboard works. *Caccia* (1978) is taken from the third movement of *Diversions,* a set of five piano pieces that he composed in 1975. It is a monothematic work in ABA' form. The middle section simply presents the theme in a contrasting key. *The Dancing Sergeant* was originally one of the *Five Images* which were composed in 1966. The entire set was transcribed for orchestra in 1967, and the final movement was scored for band in 1979. It is an amusing caricature that should be very appealing to young audiences. Both these pieces were written with young players in mind, and should be a welcome addition to the repertoire of the public school band program.

Compositions such as *Caccia* and *The Dancing Sergeant,* as well as other music that Dello Joio has written with young players in mind, can be classified as functional music (Hindemith's Gebrauchmusik). They serve a particular purpose, namely the need for well conceived compositions that are within the attainment level of young players in public school music programs. They are a reflection of Dello Joio's philosophy that the professional composer has an obligation to satisfy this need. They also reflect the fact that he is a free-lance composer who depends on the income from his music for his livelihood. Being keenly aware of the commercial value of music that is well thought of by those in the music teaching profession, Dello Joio does not hesitate to get as much mileage as possible from an idea by transcribing his music for performance in several different media.

8

Dramatic Music

Throughout the history of Western Civilization, the dramatic arts have relied on music to fulfill certain functions that cannot be fulfilled by words and action alone. The development of this musico/dramatic relationship can be traced from the music dramas of the ancient Greeks through the medieval liturgical dramas, incidental music for the plays of Shakespeare and later playwrights, the development of opera, operetta, and musical comedy, and finally in the twentieth century to the advent of motion pictures and television. Thus, composers from all periods of Western art have been called upon to write dramatic music in one form or another, and Dello Joio is no exception. This chapter will deal with his incidental theatre music and musical scores that he has written for television and film. A separate chapter has been devoted to his operas.

Dello Joio's work yields only three examples of incidental theatre music. The first consists of music for orchestra, chorus, and soloists composed in 1953, for the production of the play *The Tall Kentuckian* by Barbara Anderson. The play was written to commemorate the founding of the city of Louisville, Kentucky. Written for a commemorative occasion such as this, the play naturally contains a good deal of pageantry. The rousing choruses, ballads, and dance music composed by Dello Joio are quite apropos. Two ballads for two part chorus and piano (*Sweet Sunny* and *Somebody's Coming*) were published separately shortly after the work's premiere in 1953.

Incidental music for Shakespeare's *Anthony and Cleopatra* was composed by Dello Joio during the summer of 1960, for a production by the American Shakespeare Festival at Stratford, Connecticut. Appearing in the lead roles were Katharine Hepburn and Robert Ryan. The music is scored for a small chamber ensemble consisting of instruments carefully selected to produce a timbre that would evoke the atmosphere of ancient Egypt—flute, piccolo, oboe, English horn, B-flat clarinet, bass clarinet, two horns in F, trombone, viola, tam tam, finger cymbals, snare drum, and tympani. The use of shifting modality and synthetic scalar material endowed with augmented seconds also contributes to the effect. Because the music of this score consists of short segments lasting anywhere from fifteen seconds to two minutes, it does not lend itself to being fashioned into a suite or separate numbers for publication. Therefore it is unlikely that the listening public will hear any of it apart from a production of the play.

Such is not the case with the music for the play *Thezmophoriazousae,* a classic Greek comedy of the fourth century B. C. written by Aristophanes. Dello Joio composed this music for a production given at Boston University in 1974, when he was serving as Dean of the School of the Arts at that institution. Contained in this score are a number of songs and dances, three of which were fashioned into a score for band entitled *Satiric Dances for a Comedy by Aristophanes* (see chapter 7). Set in the ancient world of the Mediterranean, the music contains the same type of modal dialect that is present in *Anthony and Cleopatra.*

Dello Joio's first film score was written quite early in his career. It was composed in 1943 for the film *Greentree Thoroughbred,* a documentary film about the breeding of throroughbred horses at the Whitney stables in Kentucky. The location of both the score and the film remain a mystery at this point. Therefore it is not possible to comment on the music contained therein.

It was not until 1956 that Dello Joio was once again approached about writing a film score. It was at that time that television networks were first beginning to engage contemporary composers of serious music to write background music for some of their special programs. Prior to that, as a rule, contemporary composers of serious music were heard on television only in concert programs. Therefore when the Public Affairs Department of CBS News, in cooperation with the United States Air Force, decided to produce a series of films depicting the history and development of flight and its impact on twentieth century man, they commissioned four of America's leading composers to write music for the twenty-six part series—Norman Dello Joio, Paul Creston, George Antheil, and Frank Smith.

"Air Power," as the series is called, shows every aspect of aviation against a background of changing times. "Fools, daredevils, and geniuses joust with the airplane amidst the daffiness of the Roaring Twenties. Airmen prepare for their 'rendezvous with destiny' in the Desperate Thirties. And then they fight it out gloriously in the Triumphant Forties."[1] Pioneers of aviation history, such as Charles Lindbergh, Eddie Rickenbacker, and Jimmy Doolittle, are naturally brought into the story of flight. With the battles of World War II playing such a prominent role, political figures such as Winston Churchill, Franklin Delano Roosevelt, and Dwight Eisenhower are also intertwined in the narrative.

To write music for such a wide panorama of history and flight, the producers originally thought that several composers would be needed. "One alone, they felt, could not help but repeat himself in the course of the long series of films."[2] However, after hearing Dello Joio's audition score for the series, the producers found it to be so superior to what they had expected that they abandoned their original idea of having several composers, and commissioned Dello Joio to compose the music for all twenty-two of the remaining films in the series. An office with a piano and moviola was set up for him at CBS studios, and he went down every afternoon for almost a year to view the films and work on the scores. He not only wrote the music, he also did the orchestration. Ordinarily the task of scoring the music would have been turned over to a staff arranger, but in this case Dello Joio did it himself. He heard one example of the arranger's scoring and found it to be so alien to what he would have done that he rejected the idea of having someone else do the scoring.

This being only Dello Joio's second attempt at writing for film, he naturally felt somewhat constrained by the restricting confines of the medium. However, his lack of experience in this medium turned out to be an advantage because he did not feel bound by its traditions. In a New York Philharmonic Intermission Interview taped shortly after the series premiered on 11 November 1956, Dello Joio stated:

When I was first approached to do the music for this series of films, I had to think very carefully in terms of what I felt I, a writer whose whole career has been built in terms of abstract music, how to find means whereby I could give a real expression of my own, because I feel that there is a great deal of music written for movies that doesn't have very much profile. As a composer I never felt very content that I should follow along those same paths. I went ahead and tried to do things that were not usual in the accepted standard procedures as far as film writing was concerned. An example of that is one of the scenes that takes place in Berchtesgarten. Hitler and Goering are loc̲ ̲ng over a map and talking. From the film itself it was obvious they were very intense in the plans they were laying out for the possible invasion of Britain. Now this whole thing struck me as an opportunity to do something quite different. I decided to do something whereby this colloquy took place purely with percussion instruments—just an incessant kind of thing that went on between drums, cymbals, and snare drums. The total effect when it was over I think proved my point.[3]

On the television program "Profile of a Composer" Dello Joio commented further on the problem that a composer of abstract music faces when he writes film music, and explained the approach that he took in dealing with this problem.

The first rule of background music for film is that it must never be heard. Writing music for films is extremely difficult, in many ways more difficult than writing for ballet. At least in ballet the composer sets the tempo. But in films the tempos are set by the editor, by the camera itself. Last year I did a series of scores for the television program "Air Power," and one particular film dealt with a single raid—a defeat for the American Air Forces in the skies above Schweinfurt, Germany. The plot is not important. This film is about a group of men who went to die in the air above Schweinfurt. Yet it was made fourteen years after the raid. I could no longer write anything like "Nothing Can Stop the Army Air Corps." This is a documentary which means the music must be submerged even further. The shots are real. The sound effects are real. Music could be solely a comment. Here three hundred bombers begin to take off. The motion picture camera becomes repetitive and inadequate at this point. It cannot capture the sheer weight of three hundred bombers and three thousand men going out to do uncertain battle. But the editor makes a try for tempo. He begins with long shots of the airplanes; then he increases the tempo by taking closer scenes and cutting them more quickly. The tempo of the film is established by him, not by me. What the documentary camera cannot give is a point of view; a way to feel about this action.

My job is clear: set an emotional point of view with the music. Build the sense of charge and mass. But don't get away from the visual images.

There is of course, the strict craftsmanship of writing music to films. Each shot runs a certain amount of time, no longer, and I must make my music fit exactly in time.[4]

In a scene such as the one described here, Dello Joio could have projected a number of different emotional points of view. Realizing that music would be little more effective than the camera at capturing the tremendous weight of the bombers, he chose to focus on the emotions of a single individual by trying to imagine what was going through the mind of one of the pilots at a moment like this, and capturing the essence of those thoughts with the music.

Later he commented on film music in general as opposed to abstract music. "Theatrical music is only sometimes at the forefront of the art of music. At best it uses the composer's craft and skills. It always lags behind pure music as the engineer lags behind the scientist. The scientist moves into the unknown, the engineer follows him. The pure composer extends the boundaries of music, the theatrical composer follows him."[5]

Dello Joio's comment about theatrical music lagging behind pure music in artistic development is quite correct, and this applies to his own music. When a composer's primary concern is creating music to enhance a visual image, and he must do it within an externally imposed time span and meet production deadlines as well, the result is seldom going to add anything significant to the evolving language of music. At best, the composer who knows his craft will skillfully utilize the musical language that has developed up to his time. The music that Dello Joio composed for the "Air Power" series (and later scores as well), while it is done with imagination, taste, and the skill of a master craftsman, is not as advanced or modernistic in style as many examples of purely abstract music that he composed during the previous decade. The principle theme of "Air Power" (the theme that opens and closes every episode), variations of which occur during many of the episodes as a binding force for the series, gives a clue to what can be expected from the contents of the scores of "Air Power." It is quoted below with chord symbols to indicate the harmonization. It is scored for full orchestra.

Example 33. Theme from "Air Power"

Dello Joio admitted that the constant pressure to meet deadlines and the restricting confines of the film medium made the "Air Power" series his most challenging project up to that point in his career. He even described himself as a "basket case" at the end of that project. Nevertheless, the success and acclaim that the series brought him, and the lure of "big bucks" led him to explore the possibility of going to California and writing movie scores. He engaged James Pollack of Sherman Oaks, California, as an agent, and Pollack began making inquiries on Dello Joio's behalf. In August of 1959, Pollack had Stanley Kramer interested in Dello Joio for the film *Inherit the Wind,* in which Spencer Tracy played the role of Clarence Darrow at the famous Scopes Monkey Trial. However, by this time, Dello Joio had too many commitments in the East, such as an agreement with the Philadelphia Academy of Vocal Arts to write an opera, and he was unable to simply drop everything and move to the West Coast. Therefore he did not pursue the matter any further. Over the next several years however, he did write the music for a number of television films produced in New York.

In 1957, Dello Joio provided background music for a documentary film produced by CBS television entitled *Here Is New York.* The film, which is based on the off-beat writings of E. B. White, provides an inside view of the city of New York by focusing on its people. It deals with the ethnic groups, the fast paced life style of the average New Yorker, the tourists and visitors. To complement White's off-beat script, Dello Joio made abundant use of the syncopated, off-beat rhythms of jazz. Several cues incorporate a piece called the "New York Blues," scored for alto saxophone, strings, piano, and snare drum with brushes. For other cues Dello Joio used music from his 1949 suite *New York Profiles.* For the portion of the film dealing with the Italian section of New York, the last movement of that suite, called "Little Italy," seemed to be just what the film called for. Dello Joio also used segments of the movements entitled "The Park" and "The Tomb." Yet another section of the score recalls the music of "Somebody's Coming" from *The Tall Kentuckian.*

In 1960, Dello Joio wrote the music for two television films. The first was a film produced by NBC television entitled *America and Americans,* a documentary based on the writings of John Steinbeck. All of the music for this film was newly composed. An observant listener will be aware of the use of variants of a number of folk songs from Americana such as "When Those Caissons Go Rolling Along." For CBS television Dello Joio wrote the score for *Vanity Fair,* a dramatization of Thackeray's novel. Except for the use of the love theme from *The Ruby* (see chapter 9), the music for this score was also newly composed. The melody of Act I, cue 7 was later used in the set of children's piano pieces called *Family Album.*

"The Saintmaker's Christmas Eve" was a Christmas special that was broadcast by ABC television on 24 December 1961. Produced by the National Council of Catholic Men, the dramatization is based on a short story by Paul Horgan. The story concerns a Mexican peasant who carved a small wooden statue of the Christ and the miracle that occured as a result. For this score Dello Joio composed a "Lullaby to the Christ Child," which was later published as the song "The Holy Infant's Lullaby." In other sections of the score he utilized two chant melodies that he has used often in other compositions—"Kyrie" from the *Mass of Angels* and "Ite Missa Est."

Dello Joio began work on the ill-fated *Time of Decision* project in 1962. This was originally planned by producer David Susskind of Talent Associates as a series of twenty-six, one hour programs dealing with the presidential administration of Harry S Truman. Rejected by all three major networks, Susskind announced on 22 June 1961 that he would produce and finance the twenty-six programs at a cost of $2,000,000 despite the networks' lack of interest, and he commissioned Dello Joio to write the music. Subsequent decisions to cut the number of programs in the series and change to a half-hour format still did not interest any of the networks. After the production of two pilot films—"Man From Independence" and "Korean War Decision," Susskind sold his interest in the series to Screen Gems, Incorporated which completed a condensed version of the series using stock music. Thus, what was originally to have been for Dello Joio another series on the same magnitude as "Air Power," turned out to be only a single pilot film. Based on comments made to Harold Stern in an interview of 6 June 1962, it is clear that Dello Joio was at that time thinking in terms of a series, not a single program. His comments also shed some additional light on his approach to writing film scores and his method of operation which was not only planned for this series, but is evident in "Air Power" as well.

I didn't write the score from a finished product. They set up a moviola in my home and I worked along with them. . . . As soon as they have enough film for me to work with, I'll get to see it and get a copy of the script as well.

I think for the series I already have the basic theme—the Truman theme. In a series, there's generally a unifying theme. Then I block out three or four striking themes and work them into a unifying musical concept. I like to think in terms of a total concept, not in bits and pieces. There's more of a problem in this series because it deals with an individual with so many facets to his personality.

When I met Harry Truman, I discovered a personality totally different from his public image, and if I hadn't met him I'd have written an entirely different theme. He's a man of great simplicity and great firmness. As far as he's concerned, there's never a question of what's right or wrong. Spending some time with him affected my whole approach. And having him watch the opening show and fill me in on what was happening was a thrilling experience.

I had to capture the folk and simple background and combine it with the importance of the position he held. He was a president who had to make some of the most important decisions in history. I hope I've captured that.[6]

Dello Joio completed work on the pilot film in October 1962, but the program did not appear on television until 1966. The opening theme music is quoted here. The simple diatonic structure of the melody captures the simplicity of the man himself while its performance by trumpets and horns at a stately tempo relates to the dignity of the office which he held.

Example 34. Theme from *Time of Decision*

The music of the film score *From Every Horizon* is discussed in chapter 7 in connection with the band score of the same title. To avoid redundancy the reader is referred there for information concerning the composition of that score.

The most recent film score to come from Dello Joio's pen is the award-winning television special "The Louvre," which premiered on NBC television on 17 November 1964. (A sixteen millimeter film produced by Encyclopedia Britannica Films is available on rental from most major film libraries in the United States.) Produced by Lucey Jarvis and John Sughrue, "The Louvre" captured the 1965 Emmy Awards for directing, writing, editing, cinematography, and music. The film focuses on the palace building in Paris and its world famous art collection as a "summation of national history and a symbol of French culture."[7] It traces the history of the palace, the people who lived in it, and who helped build its collections, such as Henry II, Marie di Medici, Louis XIV, and Napoleon Bonaparte. Included in the film is a scale model that narrator Charles Boyer takes apart and puts back together like a child's construction set to give the viewer a better look at the building's complex structure.

To complement the scenes in this film, Dello Joio selected many of his themes from the music of composers who were contemporary with the persons and events under discussion. The section on Louis XIV, for example, is based on Jean Baptiste Lully's (1632–87) "Chaconne aus der Oper Roland."[8] Lully was court composer to the boy king. Scored for an ensemble of oboe, trumpets in C, French horn, trombone, organ and strings, the music has a true baroque flavor. Other themes were selected because they captured the mood needed to enhance a particular scene. The music for the grotesque drawing of the infamous massacre of Saint Bartholomew's Day in the Tuilleries courtyard (24 August 1572) is based on Jan Petersz Sweelinck's (1562–1621) *Fantasia Chromatica für Orgel oder Klavier* (GMB#158). Sweelinck's theme and Dello Joio's arrangement of it are quoted in example 35.

Example 35a. Sweelinck, *Fantasia Chromatica* (GMB #158)

Example 35b. Dello Joio, *The Louvre,* cue 5

The descending chromatic line played at a slow tempo creates an appropriate feeling of remorse. By way of contrast, the twenty-one giant paintings by Peter Paul Rubens, which were commissioned to illustrate the glories of the reign of Marie di Medici (1573–1642), are characterized musically by this assertive theme of Adriano Banchieri (c. 1565–1634).

Example 36. Banchieri, *Sinfonia d'istromenti senza voci*

Not all of the music for *The Louvre* is transcribed. The title music and many of the shorter cues are original with Dello Joio, but blended well with the remainder of the score and always consistent with the theme of the visual cues they accompany—a waltz in nineteenth style to highlight the accomplishments of Napoleon III, and music with an impressionistic tinge to compliment the paintings of Claude Monet.

The music of *The Louvre* is a testimony to Dello Joio's keen sense of the theatrical as it reveals throughout his uncanny ability to divulge the appropriate musical response to every visual image. It also reveals some of the reasons behind the point cited earlier, that theatrical music always lags behind pure music in terms of the evolution of musical style. The fact that a score such as this was judged as the outstanding accomplishment in its field for the year in which it was done, is an indication that the producers and critics of film music are not at all concerned with the advancement or uniqueness of the musical language of a film score, but only with its suitability for the visual image it is intended to enhance.

9

Operas

Dello Joio's endeavors in the operatic genre have met with both success and frustration. In his efforts to achieve success as an opera composer, a number of factors were in his favor. First, there is the matter of his Italian heritage. Opera was born in Italy almost four hundred years ago and has had an unbroken tradition there since its inception. Although Dello Joio's ancestors were church musicians rather than opera composers, he did inherit from them an Italianate love of melody. That, combined with his early experience of listening to the opera singers who came to his father for coaching, and his frequent attendance at the opera house as a youth, gave him a natural feeling for writing melody that is singable and vocally gratifying. His knowledge of Gregorian chant gained through his own experience as a church organist in the Roman Catholic church also contributed to his feel for natural rhythmic and melodic flow. His broad acquaintance with operatic as well as dramatic literature enabled him to develop a sense of theatricality—what would work and what would not work on the operatic stage. With that kind of background it was inevitable that once his compositional craft developed to the point that he could handle extended instrumental forms successfully, he would try his hand at composing an opera. However, before that could be attempted, two critical problems had to be solved. He had to find suitable dramatic material that would inspire his best efforts, and he had to find a librettist who could provide him with a text that would allow his musico-dramatic instinct to function at its best. Those two problems have been a constant source of frustration. For years dating back as early as 1959, he has had a strong desire to write an opera based on Hemingway's *For Whom the Bell Tolls*, but has never been able to get permission from

Hemingway's widow to extract a libretto. His collaborative efforts with the librettists Joseph Machlis, William Gibson, and Gale Hoffman resulted in his having to rewrite, have rewritten, or discard much of the material provided.

Another source of frustration for Dello Joio and all contemporary American composers in the infrequency with which professional opera companies in this country perform contemporary operas. He pinned a great deal of hope on the outcome of the San Francisco Opera's performances of *Blood Moon* in 1961. The Metropolitan Opera had tentative plans for subsequent performances if the San Francisco premiere proved successful. Successful premieres in San Francisco and New York would likely have brought commissions for additional operas from his pen. Those hopes were dashed by the critics, or more probably one in particular. After the *New York Times* printed a scathing review by Alan Rich in which he described *Blood Moon* as "threadbare, overlong, and downright boring,"[1] the Met lost interest. Reviewing a Los Angeles performance by the same cast, Clyde Leech wrote, "*Blood Moon* . . . appears, even at first hearing, to possess qualities that should entitle it to a place of permanent recognition in the world centers of opera."[2] One wonders if the Met might not have gotten cold feet if Mr. Leech's review had appeared in New York rather than Mr. Rich's. In the face of such difficulties, it is not surprising to find that a composer with the lyric gift and sound dramatic instincts of Dello Joio has written only four operas to date.

The first dramatic subject that Dello Joio chose as the basis of an opera was Joan of Arc, and he was so consumed by it that it occupied him off and on for a period of ten years beginning in 1949. He was not the first to be inspired by the maid of Lorraine. The image of Joan of Arc has for centuries challenged creative minds to probe into the meaning of her life and try to project that through artistic expression. Shakespeare, Schiller, Shaw, Verdi, Tchaikovsky, and Honneger are but a few of the more prominent figures who have wrestled with the subject of the maid. Dello Joio was a boy of twelve when he first encountered Joan. "One day, while in the organ loft, I happened upon a picture book of the lives of the saints. I read for the first time of the maid from Lorraine and since that still vivid meeting with the girl, she has played to this day an important role in my musical thinking and career."[3] During the years following that initial encounter, Dello Joio spent many hours reading about some aspect of St. Joan and discovered that the literature on her was enormous. Eventually he came to his own conclusions about the meaning of her life. "Firmly, I perceived that the timelessness and universality of Joan as a symbol lay in the eternal problem of the individual's struggle to reconcile his personal beliefs with what he is expected to believe. Daily, for ages, she has challenged men to have her courage; and, as in the past, she will always serve as a continual source of reference for the artist. In a sense she epitomizes his struggle—fulfillment by sacrifice."[4]

With Joan exercising such a profound influence on Dello Joio, it is not surprising to discover her as the subject of his first opera, *The Triumph of Joan*, which he composed during 1949–50 while on the faculty at Sarah Lawrence College. He had been searching for suitable material for an opera for some time, and when the administration at Sarah Lawrence expressed a desire to integrate the performing arts departments with a project that would give each department—music, theatre, and dance—an integral part in the whole production, something was bound to happen. A two-thousand dollar grant from the Whitney Foundation enabled the college to commission Dello Joio to write the work as well as cover production costs. What turned out to be the deciding factor in making Joan the subject of the opera was the 1949 film *Joan of Arc*, which featured Ingrid Bergman in the title role. The film accurately portrayed the events of Joan's life—her humble beginnings as a shepherdess in Domremy, her courageous leadership of the French army, the coronation of Charles VII, her arrest, trial and execution as a sorceress. Dello Joio and Joseph Machlis, music instructor at Queens College, saw the film and agreed that its externality suggested a parallel story dealing with the inner motivations and spiritual life of Joan. The two of them collaborated in fashioning a libretto with the composer selecting what he wanted and discarding the rest. The result was an opera in three acts with three scenes each:

> Act I, Scene 1—A cell in the fortress at Rouen
> Scene 2—A forest clearing near Domremy
> Scene 3—The palace of the Dauphin at Chinon
> Act II, Scene 1—The cell
> Scene 2—Before the wall of Orleans
> Scene 3—The Coronation at Rheims
> Act III, Scene 1—The court of Charles VII at Poitiers
> Scene 2—The trial at Rouen
> Scene 3—The cell

The cast calls for three principals—Joan, the Dauphin, and the Bishop of Beauvais, six speaking roles, women's chorus, and dancers. The scenes in the cell take place immediately after Joan's trial in the year 1431. In the other scenes, the principal events in Joan's life are reconstructed in a series of flashbacks.

In keeping with his charge to provide a work that would give all departments an integral part in the production, Dello Joio constructed the work in a way that gives not only the principals, but everyone in the cast a legitimate role to play in the drama. The members of the chorus, in addition to being active participants in the court, coronation, and trial scenes, also function in the manner of the ancient Greek chorus as audience interpreter. They see the things that go through Joan's mind as she is trying to come to some conclusions about herself, and reflect these to the audience. The dances are an expression of certain situations that occur dramatically and could only be developed through dance.

The main musical interest lies, as it does in most operas, in the set numbers—the maid's soliloquy, the Bishop's creed, and Joan's duet with the Dauphin. Here Dello Joio's lyric gift is allowed to develop fully. However, the use of spoken dialogue and whispered choruses, while serving a dramatic purpose, does hinder the musical development. Also, the use of the flashback technique impedes the logical progression to a dramatic climax through music. In spite of these structural flaws, the work did receive a considerable amount of praise from some of the leading critics in New York. Dello Joio, however, was not satisfied that the opera said all that he wanted to say about Joan, and refused offers to publish the score. Instead, he took thematic material from the preludes to each of the three acts, and set to work composing *The Triumph of Saint Joan Symphony* (see chapter 3).

Although the symphony was a very successful work, Dello Joio was still not satisfied that he had captured the essence of Joan in music. He embarked on a lengthy study of the legal proceedings that sent Joan to the stake in 1431. He wrote a new libretto based on the written record of the trial, and titled his new opera *The Trial at Rouen*. This work was premiered on NBC Television on 8 April 1956. In it the composer focuses on the events of the trial and the final phases of Joan's life. Past episodes are revealed only through conversation. Although the opera is written in two acts of two scenes each, the television production played them through without interruption: Bishop Pierre Cauchon and Friar Julien in a council room, Julian (Joan's confessor) and Joan in her cell, then the main body of the work in the trial chamber, and finally Joan at the stake. The pretrial scenes in the first act serve to delineate the principle characters in the drama and draw the essential line of conflict. The act closes on a dramatic high point with the maid's soliloquy in which she struggles to find the answer to her fate—will she don a dress and return to her life as a simple maid, or will she continue on her present course which can lead to only one end, death by fire? Act II opens with a delightfully effective chatter chorus for the populace as they push their way past the guards into the trial chamber. The Bishop's creed, the dramatic rejoinder to the maid's soliloquy, then sets the tone for the remainder of the scene as the opera moves with sustained dramatic power to the climactic point at which Joan breaks under the pressure of the Inquisition and recants. At this point time is suspended in the midst of a total blackout on stage except for a single pin spot on Joan. She struggles mightily as her inner voice seeks the meaning of life. Here, instead of using the device of the whispered chorus to reflect Joan's inner thoughts, Dello Joio resorts to a single voice that is either projected through a microphone or prerecorded. As Joan calls for her "inner voices" they are heard from off stage (Soprano, Alto, Tenor soli) bidding Joan to "Pass through the fire to the eternal reward that now awaits you." The meaning is now clear; she can gain freedom only through martyrdom. The scene at the stake then is dramatically and musically anticlimactic, for Joan's struggle was to discover the true meaning of her existence. From the moment that became clear, she was no longer afraid to face the fire.

Armed with a libretto that was much more compact and intense than the earlier version of Joan, Dello Joio was able to realize his original aim of focusing the audience's attention on Joan's inner struggle rather than the external events that surrounded it. The essential musical material is drawn from the earlier opera and the symphony, but it has been reworked in a way that draws stronger characters and gives new meaning to the dramatic situations. Just as he does in the introduction to many of his instrumental works, Dello Joio outlines the main motives of the opera in the brief prelude to Act I. The difference is that here the motives have dramatic significance that go beyond mere musical meaning. The principal motive of the opera (example 37a) is sounded in the first bar. It may be called the fate motive because it recurs time and again to remind the audience of the fate that is in store for Joan. It occurs primarily in the orchestra, but on certain occasions in the voice line as well. For example, Bishop Cauchon's line "I condemn you to burn at the stake" (bars 632–33) is set to the notes of this motive. All subsequent motives (examples 37b, c, and d) that carry dramatic significance are related to the fate motive by their common dependence on the interval of the minor third, and their principal function is to define the character of Joan—the maid, the warrior, and the saint. Motive 37b may be called the tender maid

motive. It has the dual purpose of characterizing Julien as a compassionate, sympathetic father confessor who would rather see Joan return to
the simple life of a maid than challenge the authority of the church, as
well as reminding the audience of Joan's humble beginnings as a shepherdess. Motive 37*c* is the warrior motive. It is sounded whenever there
is reference to Joan's role as leader of the French Army. Finally, motive
37*d* is the saint motive. It is the principle melody of the three heavenly
voices that call Joan to sainthood in the final scene.

Example 37. *The Trial at Rouen,* principle motives

One additional motive (example 38) should be mentioned. This motive
consists of the first four notes of the "Kyrie" theme from the *Mass of
Angels* (example 10). Beginning in bar 268 of Act I, it is part of an orchestral accompaniment that is borrowed directly from *Meditations on
Ecclesiastes.* In that work it was associated with the text "A time to be
born." In the present work it is associated with the idea of Joan's salva-
tion (rebirth) in the eyes of the church.

Example 38. *The Trial at Rouen,* Act I, bars 268–70

The vocal writing in *The Trial at Rouen* is conditioned by two factors, one rhythmic and one melodic. The controlling rhythmic factor is the composer's sensitivity to the natural prosaic rhythm of speech. The melodic factor is his broad acquaintance and experience with Gregorian chant. In a style that ranges from dramatic recitative through arioso to the formalized expressive melody of the set numbers, the movement is primarily conjunct and diatonic within the confines of one of the church modes. The modal coloring in particular is effective in setting the period of the opera. This is established immediately following the Act I prelude as the Inquisitors chant in two-part parallel organum.

Dello Joio's means of characterization are subtle, yet effective. The opening scene between Cauchon and Julien is a good example. Here the composer is faced with a task similar to that of Verdi in the scene between King Philip and the Grand Inquisitor in *Don Carlo*, extended dialogue between two low male voices. Denied the opportunity to use timbral and registral differences, Dello Joio draws an effective profile of each character—the arrogant, uncompromising Bishop and the compassionate Friar—with subtle contrasts in the type of melodic motion in the voice line, degree of dissonance, and tonal area of the accompaniment (example 39).

Contrasting tonal areas are also used to define larger structural components in the opera. The work as a whole is in A minor, the tranquil ending on C major being a natural consequence of Joan's having at last found peace. Within that larger framework, each new dramatic situation is marked by a shift of tonal center. For example, in Act I, the entrance of the Bishop is marked by a shift from A to D, and the scene in the jail cell opens in E. A similar pattern occurs in Act II. The prelude centers on A, but the tonal center shifts to E for the Bishop's creed. It is evident

Example 39. *The Trial at Rouen*, Act I, bars 59–64

Cauchon (fearful)

formed in-to a gen-tle mo-des-ty. Be - ware of pi - ty, be - ware, the

Prince of ev - il finds sub-tle ways to shroud us in his dark-ness. He

then that tonic-dominant relationships exist between large blocks of harmonic content. However, the music does not progress functionally from chord to chord. Instead, chords are selected to produce a specific color or degree of dissonance in accordance with the textual and dramatic situation. All twelve tones are used freely to produce a specific effect. Seldom does Dello Joio restrict himself harmonically to the notes of a single key or mode. However, as mentioned earlier, he is more restrictive in his choice of notes to create lines for the voices.

Upon examination of *The Trial at Rouen,* it would appear that Dello Joio had finally solved for himself the problem of how to treat Joan through musical expression. The ingredients were all present for a successful opera—an historically true to life libretto with believable dramatic situations, well developed characters, truly expressive vocal writing, and a score that is technically and stylistically sound. Although the opera was not originally intended for television, it evidently played well in that medium, for the vast majority of critics gave it good marks. However, Dello Joio was not yet ready to terminate his relationship with Joan. For the

1959 stage production by the New York City Opera, the title was changed to *The Triumph of Saint Joan,* and three alterations were made in the score. The first was the addition of an opening aria by an English sentry who yearns to be back home with his lover. Although it is an effective musical number, it is not sufficiently relevant to the plot to justify its inclusion. The second addition was the expansion of Joan's recantation from a brief eight bar statement in dramatic recitative to an extended number endowed with histrionics, a more fitting climax to the lengthy build-up of tension that occurs during the trial scene. The third change was the addition of a farewell aria for Joan at the stake. This also proved to be a welcome addition. In *The Trial at Rouen* Joan simply marches to the stake, holds a crucifix to her breast and murmurs the words "Jesus, my Jesus" as she gazes heavenward—not sufficient to express the joy and sense of relief that she must have felt after having at last found the true meaning of her inner voices. The farewell aria provided that needed outpouring of lyrical expression to bring the opera to a successful conclusion.

At this point it is necessary to regress chronologically to 1952, the year in which Dello Joio began work on his second opera, *The Ruby.* He first conceived the idea after reading the play *A Night at an Inn,* by Lord Dunsany. Dunsany's play is the last of a sequence of four one-act plays collectively titled *Plays of Gods and Men. A Night at an Inn* concerns four English merchant seamen—A. E. Scott-Fortescue (The Toff), William Jones (Bill in the play, changed to Bull in the opera), Albert Thomas, and Jacob Smith (Sniggers)—who scale the heights of a mountain in Asia to steal a giant ruby from the eye of a stone idol. They succeed in smuggling it back to their lodge on the English moors, but are followed by three Priests of Klesh who seek to avenge this sacrilegious crime and return the ruby to the idol. The smugglers set a trap and slay the three priests, but their sense of relief is short lived. Klesh (the idol itself) enters the room, reclaims its eye and exits. The seamen are then drawn through the door one by one by some mysterious magnetic force.

For this opera, Dello Joio collaborated with his friend William Gibson, a novelist and playwright. Work began on the libretto during the summer of 1952, and the score was completed 9 November 1953. The world premiere took place on 13 May 1955 at Indiana University. The road to completion was not a smooth one. Correspondence between composer and librettist indicates that there was substantial disagreement concerning language, psychological development of characters, setting, and major dramatic events. Gibson took for granted that Dello Joio would delete anything that he felt would not sing. However, the text that was finally adopted was so different from what Gibson had written that he insisted it be published under a pseudonym (thus the name William Mass appears in the published score). At one point Dello Joio wanted to place more emphasis on Scott's mental condition and have him go completely insane at the end. But, in the final solution he remains essentially the type of character that Dunsany created—somewhat delusional, but always able to deal with reality. On another occasion Gibson suggested giving the opera a real American tinge by transferring the setting to the New Mexico desert, making the characters Americans, and updating the time to the present (1953). That idea was rejected and the place and time remained on the English moors around the turn of the century. At Dello Joio's suggestion, the character of Laura, Scott's wife, was introduced. He felt there needed to be some break in the mounting dramatic tension, and a romantic reunion between the pair of lovers would provide that. The point of disagreement was over the eventual fate of Laura. Dello Joio's idea was to have her killed either by the priests or by the smugglers in rebellion against Scott. Gibson argued strongly against that solution and his opinion prevailed. Laura is the only character left alive at the end of the opera. Dello Joio and Gibson debated the idea of a plot devoid of the idol. Gibson felt that although the idea of an idol that takes its own revenge was hokey, without it, the story had no touch of originality. Thus the idol remained. After these extensive deliberations, the libretto on which they finally settled, with the exception of Laura, parallelled the events of Dunsany's play exactly.

The result of this collaborative effort was a music drama that has all the characteristics of a seething melodrama. The excited conversation of the thieves is set in a highly concentrated form of dramatic recitative with the accompaniment providing an almost literal description of every word and action. A consistently dissonant harmonic language keeps the air filled with tension throughout the dramatic opening and closing scenes. The interval content of the two chords that set the stage for the opening scene is typical (example 40). The bichordal structure of these two harmonic entities, consisting of two different chords (d/D + 7 Bb/b) both with the same root in the case of the former, and roots one half step apart in the case of the latter, creates dissonant minor second clashes between multiple chord members. The implications of the harmonic minor second are realized in the frequent chromatic movement of the voice lines (example 41).

The only relief from this extreme dissonance and chromaticism comes

Example 40. *The Ruby,* bar 17

Example 41. *The Ruby,* fig. 3, bars 1–4

during the love scene between Scott and Laura. At that point the emphasis shifts to the consonant third (example 42), thirds in the context of seventh and ninth chords. A shift to a harmonic language consisting of plain triads would be too abrupt and stylistically inconsistent with the score as a whole. The vocal writing in this scene changes from the conversational to a kind of lyricism reminiscent of Verdi and Puccini.

Example 42. *The Ruby,* fig. 37, bars 4–5

The musical structure of *The Ruby* reveals the same economy of means found in Dello Joio's instrumental works. The entire opera is constructed from three thematic cells that are outlined in the opening bars. There is a theme of fear (example 43*a*), a theme of love (example 43*b*), and a chord which portrays the ruby (example 43*c*).

Example 43. *The Ruby,* thematic cells

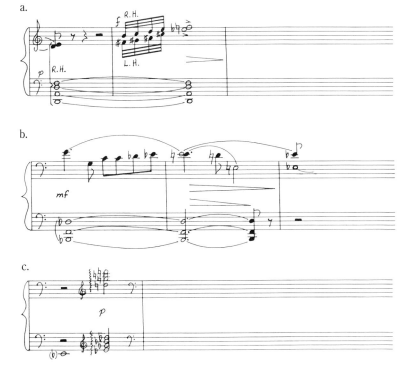

The fear motive, with its parallel scale figures (one pentatonic, the other phrygian) converging on the dissonant second, is particularly prominent when the priests enter the lodge and when the idol appears to take its vengeance. Example 44 illustrates the variety of melodic ideas that Dello Joio derives from the love motive during the duet between Scott and Laura. Here they are transposed to the same pitch level so that the relationship is more easily seen.

Example 44. *The Ruby,* derivatives of the love motive

The "Ruby chord" recurs in its original as well as various altered forms, but always with the same bichordal root relationship (G/eb7) whenever anyone comes into physical contact with the jewel. By the skillful and imaginative manipulation of the three musical ideas, Dello Joio was able to create a score that matches the libretto in terms of its intense focus on two of the most basic human emotions—fear and love—and endow the entire drama with an appropriate mystical atmosphere.

Dello Joio began work on his next opera, *Blood Moon,* in the spring of 1958. Having achieved success and critical acclaim for *The Ruby* and *The Trial at Rouen,* he was searching for a suitable love story as the subject of his first full-length opera when he happened on the story of Ada Isaacs Mencken, a young octoroon actress who achieved notable fame in the theatres of this country during the mid-nineteenth century, but whose mixed blood caused her considerable trouble. He developed his own scenario and sent copies to Max Rudolf who was at that time artistic director of the Metropolitan Opera, and Kurt Herbert Adler, general manager of the San Francisco Opera, soliciting their opinion as to its suitability for an opera and their willingness to produce the work upon its completion. Both expressed an interest in the ultimate outcome, but neither was willing to make a commitment at that point. Dello Joio then engaged Gale Hoffman to write the libretto. In October of 1958, Dello Joio signed a contract with the Academy of Vocal Arts in Philadelphia to occupy a chair in composition and write a one-act opera to be completed by 1 October 1959. At first he contemplated a one-act comic opera called *The Ringmaster,* but in February of 1959, he received approval from the Academy's Board of Directors to extend the libretto of *The Ringmaster* to a two or three act opera. Subsequently he received approval to abandon *The Ringmaster* altogether and substitute Hoffman's libretto based on the Mencken story. The music of the first act was completed by 1 October 1959 and a good deal of the second act was done by March of 1960. Spurred by the Ford Foundation's generous offer to subsidize the production of new American operas, the Metropolitan Opera, the Chicago Lyric Opera, and the San Francisco Opera all expressed an interest in premiering Dello Joio's new opera. San Francisco ultimately succeeded in getting first performance rights and scheduled the work for the opening of its fall 1961 season. Dello Joio completed work on the score in April of that year, and the world premiere took place on September 18.

Blood Moon is a love story, not unlike that of Alfredo and Violetta in *La traviata,* in which the two lovers are prevented from finding true happiness together because of the conventions and prejudices of society. In this case it is racial prejudice. The setting is in New Orleans, New York, and Paris during the years immediately preceding the United States Civil War. The opera's principal character, Ninette LaFont, is a beautiful young octoroon actress who has managed to keep the facts about her ancestry a secret. As the bright new star of the New Orleans stage, she has attracted the attention of Raymond Bardac, a wealthy young Creole. Her quadroon mother, Cleo, was spied upon and severely beaten because of her love affair with Ninette's father, and is determined that Ninette will never become involved with a white man. At a party at the Bardac estate, Edmee LeBlanc, Ninette's rival both in love and on stage, discovers her secret and threatens to expose her if she does not leave New Orleans. Knowing her career and her relationship with Raymond would be ruined if her secret was revealed, Ninette agrees and she and Cleo depart. Undaunted, Raymond pursues her first to New York, and then to Paris where she has become the leading lady for Alexander Dumas, who was himself reputedly of mixed blood. When Cleo interferes with Raymond's attempt to persuade Ninette to marry him and return to New Orleans, he becomes so enraged that he calls her a black witch and attempts to strike her, only to be held back by Dumas. This action forces Ninette to face reality and reveal that Cleo is not her maid, but her mother. A stunned Raymond then proposes to remain in Paris and marry her anyway. Ninette, however, will not allow him to sacrifice his honor for her sake and convinces him that he must return to his homeland and fight for that which he believes. As for herself, she has finally discovered true freedom by admitting who she really is and refusing to live a lie any longer.

To attempt to couch this story in lyrical terms and present it on the operatic stage at that particular moment in the history of this country took no small amount of courage on the part of Dello Joio, for the race issue was at a flash point. It was in 1957 that President Eisenhower sent federal troops into Little Rock to enforce the 1954 Supreme Court decision barring segregation in the public schools. The first civil rights marches led by Martin Luther King took place in the early sixties. Governors of two southern states personally blocked the paths of black students attempting to enroll at previously all-white state universities, and young civil rights workers attempting to organize and register black voters in the South were slain. Operating in that kind of socio-political atmosphere, Dello Joio had to overcome some initial reluctance on the part of the management in San Francisco to accept for production a work such as *Blood Moon.* Writing for the *San Francisco Chronicle,* he expressed his own feelings about the social implications inherent in his subject, and their relationship to the drama as a whole:

> . . . Ninette's love for Raymond Bardac goes contrary to the conventions of society. . . . I found myself looking for someone to put on stage with whom any man could fall in love, but in so doing would be confronted with a decision about one of the perplexing problems that affect us all in this mid-twentieth century. . . . In *Blood Moon* my characters are caught up in a society and its conventions for which they cannot be individually held accountable. I have tried to present things as they are, not as I would wish them. This is not a socially conscious opera, but simply the story of two star crossed lovers who meet, love, and part. . . . One of the difficulties in writing this opera was to strike the right note in dealing with the subject of mixed love, for if at any point the audience loses sympathy with any main characters, I have failed to achieve what I set out to do.[5]

From this statement it is evident that Dello Joio was very much aware of the pitfalls involved in writing an opera that although historically removed in time, related very strongly to one of the most significant social problems of the mid-twentiery century. It would not be easy to convince the audience that Ninette and Raymond were simply two individuals caught up in a situation bigger than both of them, expressing their own very strong emotions. If anyone felt for a moment that these were puppets used to project a message, that it wasn't the characters who were speaking, but the composer who was preaching, then the opera was doomed to failure from the start. To avoid that pitfall, Dello Joio employed a traditional operatic style with emphasis on set numbers in which the characters' emotions are projected through the lyrical quality of the music. That allows the attention of the audience to focus on the purely emotional qualities in the drama rather than any underlying morality which may be present. He described his intention as follows: ". . . . The nature of the opera's dramatic line compelled me to revert to certain traditional procedures. The aria, duet, and quartet best served to convey what I felt needed to be said. In addition, I have tried to serve the singer by writing the melodic lines in as vocally grateful a manner as I am capable of. The music is tonal, as is all of my music, but I do use the twelve tones freely within any given tonality."[6]

Unlike his earlier operas in which the dialogue and action proceed in a musically and dramatically heightened form of recitative, and extended solos were better described as soliloquy than aria, *Blood Moon* contains set numbers that function in a more traditional manner. Here, instead of merging with the rest of the dialogue in a continuous flow, the set numbers stand out in relief and allow the characters to get caught up in the grip of a single overwhelming emotion. In between the set numbers the dialogue proceeds in a vocal style ranging from secco recitative to arioso. Act II, scene 2 is a good case in point. It opens with a brief orchestral interlude which creates the illusion of the passage of time from around midnight to the predawn hours. Raymond then appears in front of Ninette's New York apartment where he finds Cleo supervising the removal of trunks for their departure to Paris. A brief dialogue ensues in which Cleo tells Raymond that Ninette is out and won't be back for several hours. He insists on waiting and during this pause in the action he expresses his love for Ninette in an extended aria that culminates on high C. Ninette returns escorted by Tom Henney, a New York politician. Following polite, formal introductions, a trio begins in which Tom and Raymond engage in a heated political argument while Ninette attempts to mediate. Tom gives Raymond a blow with his cane and is banished by Ninette. She remains to see after Raymond's wound. In an extended love duet he pleads with her to marry him and she finally yields as the two of them go off into the interior to make the ultimate pledge of love.

Throughout the opera the singing is supported by a continuous orchestral background in which motives of reminiscence are woven in and out of the orchestral fabric. The most significant of these is the "rose" theme. This theme is first stated at the opening of the prelude to Act I, and returns shortly in the opening scene as Ninette bursts into her apartment to tell Cleo of her audition at the theatre in which she sang this song:

Example 45. *Blood Moon,* Act I, Scene 1, bars 36–38

During the second act love duet between Ninette and Raymond, this theme is present in all its splendor in the orchestral accompaniment. But in Act III, when Raymond has threatened to kill Cleo and Ninette has finally come to the realization that she could never share her life with this man, the rose suddenly withers as the range of the theme is diminished by chromatic alteration (example 46).

Dello Joio's emphasis on extremely lyrical, ingratiating melodies surrounded by the mildest form of dissonance led some critics to accuse him

Example 46. *Blood Moon,* Act III, fig. 47

of being old-fashioned, and there is no question that melodically, harmonically, and orchestrally, it would be difficult to be more Romantic. However, when viewed in the light of his entire operatic output to date, the score of *Blood Moon* yields a slightly different perspective. It reveals a part of the composer's artistic credo, and that is his belief that music is a means of expressing human feelings and emotions, and that the composer is free to choose the musical materials that he feels are most capable of achieving the intended expression. *The Ruby* demonstrated that when it suits his dramatic purpose, Dello Joio can write in a harshly dissonant, modernistic style. However, as that statement implies, he doesn't do it just for the sake of being modern. Neither does he write in a decidely Romantic style just for the sake of being old-fashioned. When two reasonably sane characters are expressing sincere, passionate feelings toward each other, it is difficult for Dello Joio to imagine those feelings being realistically expressed in the angular, atonal style of the Schoenberg-Berg-Webern school or any of the more recent avant-garde types of musical expression. That style is appropriate and highly effective for the demented characters encountered in *Wozzeck* and *Lulu,* but not for the characters in *Blood Moon.* Therefore it should come as no surprise that in an opera in which the dominant theme is not fear, but love— love between an aristocratic Southern gentleman of the pre-Civil War era and a young actress who lives in the fantasy world of the theatre—the type of lyrical expression that provided only a brief interlude in *The Ruby* would become predominant. It becomes predominant because that is the musical language in which Dello Joio most comfortably and convincingly conveys the emotions expressed by the characters in the drama.

10

Reflections

Reflecting back on Dello Joio's career to date, it is possible to observe three fairly distinct phases. These phases are not the equivalent of what may be observed in the career of a composer such as Beethoven in which, as Maynard Solomon so ably points out, each new period of creativity is triggered by personal tragedy and severe psychological trauma.[1] Neither are they marked by a radical shift of style as may be noted in Stravinsky's movement from his early period to his neoclassic period and finally to his twelve-tone period. Instead, the phases in Dello Joio's career are marked by shifts of emphasis as each new phase opens up new creative vistas for him.

The decade of the forties was a period in which Dello Joio moved out of his training period and endeavored to establish himself as a composer of serious music to be reckoned with. The emphasis was on traditional genres of abstract music—orchestral music, chamber music, keyboard music, and a few notable examples of choral music and solo song. Having achieved notable success in each of these areas, he began to search for new challenges in the field of dramatic music. His most outstanding achievements during the decade of the fifties were in the fields of opera, music for television/film, and ballet. It was more by accident than design that Dello Joio became involved with the Ford Foundation and CMP, which ushered in the third phase of his career in which the emphasis shifted to music for the educational sphere. McNeil Lowry just happened to see Dello Joio on "Profile of a Composer," and as a result asked him to participate in preliminary discussions relative to the Ford Foundation and the arts.

These three phases of Dello Joio's career occurred not only because of his search for new creative challenges, but also because of the economic realities that must be faced by the free-lance composer in contemporary society. Until he joined the faculty at Boston University in 1972, Dello Joio never held a full-time position in the world of academe. During the five years he taught at Sarah Lawrence, he taught only two days a week. Although he was listed on the faculty at Mannes College of Music from 1956 to 1972, his contract called for him to teach only those composition students that he felt had real potential, and he never taught more than five or six students during that entire period. He accepted the challenges and the limitations that the life of a free-lance composer offered. The fact is that if he had spent his time composing master symphonies and string quartets, he likely would have starved. On the other hand, the two areas that in present day society offer the composer of serious music the best chance of financial success are the television/film medium and the educational world. Dello Joio could not have been as successful as he has been if he had not confronted the challenges that these two worlds had to offer and met them successfully.

Dello Joio's line of development as a composer roughly parallels these three phases of his career, and is influenced by prevailing conditions during each phase. From his very beginnings as a composer, his musical language was rooted in the tonally based neoclassical tradition of Stravinsky and Hindemith, conditioned by the modal influence of Gregorian chant and the dynamic rhythm of jazz. Dello Joio's career is marked not by a constant searching for a new musical language, but by mastery and refinement of technique. He progressed rapidly toward that end during the first phase of his career. Works such as *Variations, Chaconne, and Finale* and *Concertante* for clarinet and orchestra reveal a composer who is extremely adept at problems of melodic construction, thematic development, and variation. During the second phase the problem that he faced was not so much one of continual advancement of his technique, but one of adaptation of an already developed musical language and technique to the demands of new media—opera and television/film. The demands of television/film in particular, with the constant pressure to meet deadlines and the strictly imposed time limitations, did not allow him the luxury of choosing a fresh language for each new work as advocated by Elliot Carter.[2] The third phase opens with the *Fantasy and Variations* for piano and orchestra, an abstract work based on a four note theme in which Dello Joio shows remarkable skill and imagination in his extremely economic use of the material at hand—a trend that has continued right up to the present. The third phase is also the period in which Dello Joio made his first excursions into the world of serial music with compositions such as *Night Song* for piano, *Colloquies* for violin and piano, and *Concertante* for wind instruments. It should be noted that even in his twelve-tone works, Dello Joio never completely abandons tonality.[3] He experimented with the technique to see what it could offer him and molded it to his own use. The language of his twelve-tone works is still unmistakably his own.

This account of Dello Joio's life, his work, and what it has meant to the American public would not be complete if I did not convey some of my personal impressions of the man that I have come to know not only through his music and his writing, but also through the face to face encounter that I had with him during the four weeks I spent in his home in the process of researching this manuscript.

The man that I met is a very open, warm human being who shared with me the material benefits of his home, the aura and mystique of the attic studio where he composes and where he houses well over one-hundred manuscripts that are the result of his life's work. He readily revealed his attitudes and feelings about life, art, and the world in which we live. I could not help but be impressed by the intensity of his feelings. He is a man of principle who is firmly committed to his own manner of artistic expression while at the same time advocating freedom of expression for those who would choose other means. The sincere expression of emotion and the simple, easily comprehendible style of his music is a reflection of the kind of life he advocates—"an artistic way of life in which each person can rediscover the grace that can go into life, the joy of doing something for itself whether building a cabinet or composing a work of art."[4]

Notes and References

Chapter 1

1. Taped interview with Norman Dello Joio, 18 November 1979. Tape in possession of the author.

2. Until 1963, when the *Constitution on Sacred Liturgy* issued by the Vatican Council provided for a change to the vernacular, the liturgy was still performed in Latin, and Gregorian chant was very much in use.

3. "Profile of a Composer," script of the television program provided by Norman Dello Joio.

4. Robin Sabin, "Norman Dello Joio," *Musical America,* 1 December 1950, p. 9.

5. Norman Dello Joio, "Some Random Thoughts on Music," unpublished lecture delivered at Boston University, p. 4.

6. Ibid., pp. 3–4.

7. "Profile of a Composer."

8. Ibid.

9. Sabin, "Norman Dello Joio," p. 9.

10. Donald Fuller, "Bernard Wagenaar, a Protrait," *Modern Music* 21, no. 4 (May–June 1944): 225–31.

11. Joan Peyser, *The New Music* (New York, 1971), p. 115.

12. Ibid., p. 124.

13. Ibid., p. 157.

14. Ibid., p. 166.

15. Ibid.

16. L. Horst, "Composer/Choreographer," *Dance Perspectives,* no. 16 (1963): 18.

17. Saint Louis Symphony Broadcast, 13 June 1982.

18. Peyser, *New Music,* p. 165.

19. Norman Dello Joio, "The Composer in Society," lecture delivered at University of Hawaii, 21 April 1966. Taped copy in possession of the author.

20. Dello Joio, "Random Thoughts," pp. 7–8.

21. Taped interview with Norman Dello Joio, 20 November 1979. Tape in possession of the author.

22. Raymond Erickson, "He Believes in the Creator," *New York Times,* 9 July 1972, II, 9:1.

23. *Boston Sunday Globe,* 17 December 1972, B, pp. 39–40.

24. Martin Cooper, ed., *New Oxford History of Music,* vol. 10, *The Modern Age,* ed. Martin Cooper (London: Oxford University Press, 1974), pp. 622–23.

25. Telephone interview with William Schuman, 29 February 1984.

26. Telephone interview with Grant Beglarian, 18 April 1984.

27. *New Oxford History of Music,* Vol. 10, pp. 623–24.

28. Ibid.

29. Telephone interview with William Schuman, 29 February 1984.

30. Telephone interview with Grant Beglarian, 18 April 1984.

31. Harold C. Schonberg, "Our Changing Musical Language," *New York Times,* 31 January 1965, p. 57.

Chapter 2

1. John Wannamaker, "The Musical Settings of Walt Whitman," (Ph.D. diss., University of Minnesota, 1975).

2. Letter from Norman Dello Joio to the author, 30 March 1980.

3. Wannamaker, "Musical Settings," p. 103.

4. Cleveland Rogers and John Block, eds., *The Gathering of Forces* (New York: Knickerbocker Press, 1920), p. 345.

5. Emory Holloway and Ralph Adlmari, eds., *New York Dissected* (New York: Rufus Rockwell Wilson Co., 1936), p. 23.

6. Taped interview with Norman Dello Joio, 20 November 1979. Tape in possession of the author.

7. For a more thorough study of the poetico-musical relationships in Dello Joio's Whitman settings, the reader is referred to the Wannamaker dissertation cited above.

8. Walt Whitman, *Leaves of Grass,* eds. Harold W. Blodgett and Sculley Bradley (New York: New York University Press, 1965), p. 409.

9. Ibid., pp. 468–69.

10. Ibid., pp. 138–39.

11. Wannamaker, "Musical Settings," p. 301.

12. This same motive also plays a significant role in the opera *The Trial at Rouen* (see chapter 9).

13. *New York Profiles* (1949) is also based on this motive (see chapter 5).

14. The author's doctoral treatise, "The Solo Vocal Works of Norman Dello Joio," is the only in-depth investigation of these works to date. While it remains unpublished, it is available from University Microfilms, Ann Arbor, Michigan.

15. *Gone* and *Joy* are not included in the above-mentioned treatise because they were unknown to the author at the time of its writing. The manuscripts of these two songs were found in the attic of the composer's home in East Hampton, New York, in the fall of 1979. He forgot he had written them.

16. Tichborne was executed as a member of the Babington conspiracy, which devised a plot to assassinate Queen Elizabeth and her chief ministers,

release Mary, Queen of Scots from captivity, and promote an uprising of English Catholics to coincide with the invasion of the Spanish Armada.

17. All three of the songs on Christmas themes are also available in arrangements for mixed chorus or treble choir with piano.

18. Philadelphia Orchestra Program Book, 26 August 1977, p. 35.

Chapter 3

1. Edward Downes, "The Music of Norman Dello Joio," *Musical Quarterly* 48, no. 2 (April 1962): 151–52.

2. Other composers commissioned were John Alden Carpenter, Howard Hanson, Henry Cowell, Roy Harris, and Charles Ives.

3. Pittsburgh Symphony Program Magazine, 4–6 January 1946, pp. 20–21.

4. Piano Sonata no. 3, which is based on the same theme, was composed during May of 1947, at the suggestion of the publisher, Carl Fischer. For a discussion of that work and its relationship to the present work, see chapter 6.

5. Dello Joio first made use of this theme in the unpublished concerto for two pianos and orchestra (1944).

6. Cincinnati Symphony Program Notes, 12 October 1956.

7. The work premiered under the title *Three Symphonic Dances*. Prior to its first hearing in New York, Dello Joio decided that the present title better conveyed what the piece was.

8. Boston Symphony Program Book, 18–19 March 1960, p. 1242.

9. It is not insignificant to note that these qualities also represent two different sides of the composer's personality. He remarked to me during one of my visits that his two sons had inherited opposite sides of his character. One is a musician and the other is an athlete.

10. Cleveland Orchestra Program Book, 20 October 1949, p. 113.

11. Unpublished letter from Norman Dello Joio to Carl Fischer, Inc., dated 30 October 1951. Copy contained in Dello Joio's letter file.

12. William Mootz, "Commissioned Works Given in Louisville," *Musical America,* 1 January 1952, p. 4.

13. Taped interview with Norman Dello Joio, 22 November 1979. Tape in the author's possession.

14. *Washington Post,* 10 March 1955.

15. Philadelphia Orchestra Program Magazine, 15–16 October 1954, p. 19.

16. *August Fanfare,* August 1956, p. 5.

17. Taped interview with Norman Dello Joio, 22 November 1979. Tape in the author's possession.

18. Unpublished letter from Lily Peter to Norman Dello Joio dated 26 October 1968. Contained in Dello Joio's letter file in East Hampton, New York.

19. Philadelphia Orchestra Program Magazine, 10 December 1976, p. 15.

Chapter 4

1. This same melodic idea later became the principle motive in *Song of the Open Road* (see chapter 2).
2. Charles F. Del Rosso, "A Study of Selected Solo Clarinet Literature of Four American Composers as a Basis for Performance and Teaching," (Ph.D. diss., Columbia University, 1969), p. 118.

Chapter 5

1. *Cincinnati Post and Times Star,* 9 March 1962.
2. In addition to changing the title, Dello Joio added ten bars of music (bars 53–63) and changed the meter in several bars from a quarter note pulse to a half note pulse.
3. *The Liber Usualis* (New York: Desclee Company, 1962), p. 19.
4. Ibid., p. 22.
5. To facilitate more widespread use, Dello Joio has also provided parts for flute, oboe, and clarinet which may be substituted for the recorders.
6. David Hickman, "Music Reviews," *ITG Newsletter,* October 1961, p. 16.

Chapter 6

1. Taped interview with Norman Dello Joio, 18 November 1979. Tape in the author's possession.
2. An excellent analysis of this sonata is found in Dean Luther Arlton's "American Piano Sonatas of the Twentieth Century," an unpublished Ph.D. dissertation submitted to Columbia University in 1969. I am indebted to him for his penetrating insight into this work, which has strongly influenced my own analysis.
3. A detailed comparison of the two works is contained in "A Comparative Study of the Sonata no. 3 for piano and the *Variations, Chaconne, and Finale* by Norman Dello Joio," an unpublished doctoral thesis submitted to Indiana University by J. R. Whalen in 1969.
4. Dello Joio first used this theme in the score that he wrote for the NBC-TV special, *The Louvre* (see chapter 8). It is based on Albrici's *Festliche Sonata* found in Arnold Schering's *Geschichte der Musik in Beispielen* (Leipzig: Breitkopf and Hartel, 1931), no. 214.
5. The Philadelphia Orchestra Program Magazine, September 1967, p. 22.

Chapter 7

1. J. S. Bach, *371 Four-Part Chorales* (New York: Associated Music Publishers), p. 65.
2. The program note in the published score of *Fantasies on a Theme by*

Haydn states that the theme is from a composition for piano. That is incorrect. The theme in question is the principle theme of the final movement of String Quartet, Opus 76, no. 2.

3. Norman Dello Joio, *Concertante for Wind Instruments* (New York: Marks Music Corporation, 1973), p. 2.

4. Norman Dello Joio, *From Every Horizon* (New York: Marks Music Corporation, 1965), p. 1.

5. Arnold Schering, *Geschichte der Musik in Beispielen* (Leipzig: Breitkopf and Hartel, 1931), no. 119.

6. Ibid., no. 214.

7. Norman Dello Joio, *Songs of Abelard* (New York: Marks Music Corporation, 1969), p. 2.

8. *Encyclopedia Americana,* 1964, S. V. "Abelard, Peter."

Chapter 8

1. Albert J. Elias, "TV Music by Contemporary Composers," *Etude,* November 1956, p. 22.

2. Ibid.

3. New York Philharmonic Intermission Interview with Norman Dello Joio. Exact date unknown, but sometime during the 1956–57 season. Taped copy in possession of the author.

4. "Profile of a Composer," script of the program furnished by Norman Dello Joio.

5. Ibid.

6. *Yonkers Herald Statesman,* 6 June 1962.

7. New York Times, 13 September 1965, p. 70.

8. Arnold Schering, *Geschichte der Musik in Beispielen* (Leipzig: Breitkopf & Hartel, 1931), no. 233.

Chapter 9

1. *New York Times,* 20 September 1961, p. 23.

2. *Los Angeles Herald and Express,* 9 November 1961.

3. Norman Dello Joio, "The Challenge of Joan," *New York Times,* 1 April 1956, X, 9:4.

4. Ibid.

5. *San Francisco Chronicle,* 17 September 1961.

6. Ibid.

Chapter 10

1. Maynard Solomon, *Beethoven* (New York: Schirmer Books, 1977).

2. Martin Boykan, "Elliot Carter and the Postwar Composers," in *Per-*

spectives on American Composers, ed. Benjamin Boretz and Edward T. Cone (New York: W. W. Norton, 1971), p. 216.

3. It is interesting to note that in some of their most recent compositions, avant-garde composers such as Kristof Pendereki seem to have rediscovered tonality and are reexamining it to see what it has to offer the late twentieth-century composer.

4. *Bostonia,* a publication of Boston University, Winter 1975, pp. 46–47.

Selected Bibliography

Primary Sources

Dello Joio, Norman. "The Challenge of Joan." *New York Times,* 1 April 1956, Sect. X, p. 9, col. 4.

———. "The Composer and the American Scene." *Music Journal,* 22 (March 1964): 31–32 + .

———. "The Composer in Society." Unpublished lecture delivered at the University of Hawaii, 21 April 1966. Taped copy located in composer's home in East Hampton, New York.

———. "Contemporary Music Project in Review." *Music Educators Journal,* 54 (March 1968): 41–72.

———. "Educators Conference A Tribute to Kodaly." *New York Times,* 2 August 1964, Sect. II, p. 9, col. 1.

———. "The Expanding Role of Contemporary Music in American Education." *International Music Educator,* 10 (October 1964): 342–45.

———. "The Influence of St. Joan Remains Deep and Powerful." *New York Herald Tribune,* 12 April 1959.

———. "Music in Education." Unpublished article written in August 1949. Copy located in composer's home in East Hampton, New York.

———. "The Musician-Teacher in Society." Unpublished address delivered at MENC National Convention, Atlanta, Georgia, 12 March 1972. Copy located in composer's home in East Hampton, New York.

———. "The Place of Contemporary Music in Music Education." *Inter-American Music Bulletin,* 57 (January 1967): 1–5.

Dello Joio, Norman and Perry Wolf. "Profile of a Composer." Unpublished script of the television program. Mimeographed copy located in composer's home in East Hampton, New York.

Dello Joio, Norman. "The Quality of Music." *Music Educators Journal* 48 no. 5 (April–May 1962): 33–35.

———. "Some Random Thoughts on Music." Unpublished lecture delivered at Boston University, 1972. Xeroxed copy located in composer's home in East Hampton, New York.

———. "What Is Good Music?" *New York Herald Tribune,* 18 December 1960, Sect. II, p. 3, col. 1.

————. *Complete Manuscripts, unedited.* There are 159 separate titles located in composer's home in East Hampton, New York.

Interviews with Norman Dello Joio, 18, 20, 22, 23 November 1979 and 28 July 1980. Transcribed from cassette tapes by the author. Tapes in author's possession.

Secondary Sources

Books

Austin, William. *Music in the Twentieth Century.* New York: W. W. Norton, 1966, 708 pp.

This is a comprehensive book on twentieth century music that focuses on music in Europe and the United States. It provides a good background against which to view Dello Joio's life and music.

Chase, Gilbert. *America's Music From the Pilgrims to the Present.* Revised second edition. New York: McGraw-Hill, 1966, 759 pp.

This is a comprehensive history of American music. Dello Joio is classified as an "Eclectic" (pp. 540–41).

Edwards, Arthur C. and **W. Thomas Marrocco.** *Music in the United States.* Dubuque, Iowa: Wm. C. Brown, 1968, 179 pp.

This is a concise picture of music in the United States. Dello Joio is classified as a contemporary composer who develops traditional styles (pp 120–21). He is also listed among those composers with neoclassical tendencies (p. 118).

Hindemith, Paul. *The Craft of Musical Composition.* Book 1 translated by Arthur Mendel; Book 2 translated by Otto Ortmann. London: Schott, 1945.

Hindemith was such a strong influence on Dello Joio that understanding the philosophy and theory of the older master sheds some light on Dello Joio's stylistic tendencies.

Hindemith, Paul. *A Composer's World.* Garden City, New York: Doubleday, 1961. 257 pp.

This book is valuable to anyone who wants to learn something of the composer's creative process.

Hitchcock, H. Wiley. *Music in the United States: A Historical Introduction.* Englewood Cliffs, New Jersey: Prentice-Hall, 1969, 270 pp.

Hitchcock relates Dello Joio to the Eastman group of composers (p. 213).

Machlis, Joseph. *American Composers of Our Time.* New York: Thomas Y. Crowell, 1963, 237 pp.

Machlis offers a brief biographical sketch that mentions some of Dello Joio's important works as well as influences on his musical personality (pp. 162–72).

Machlis, Joseph. *Introduction to Contemporary Music.* New York: W. W. Norton, 1961, 714 pp.

The first edition of this book is preferred because five pages are devoted to Dello Joio (pp. 554–58). The second edition gives him only a paragraph.

Persichetti, Vincent. *Twentieth Century Harmony.* New York: W. W. Norton, 1961, 287 pp.

This is a textbook on chord construction and progression dealing with both tertian and nontertion chords. It is an excellent source for anyone wishing to understand the harmony in Dello Joio's music.

Peyser, Joan. *The New Music.* New York: Dell Publishing Company, 1971, 204 pp.

This book gives the reader an excellent overview of the major currents in twentieth century music. It provides a background against which Dello Joio's music can be viewed.

Reti, Rudolf. *Tonality, Atonality, Pan-Tonality.* London: Rockliff, 1958, 166 pp.

The section on pan-tonality (pp. 59–119) is particularly applicable to Dello Joio's music. Reti's theory offers a plausible explanation of how some twentieth century composers (including Dello Joio) have moved away from traditional ways of writing tonal music without resorting to atonality or serialism.

Salzman, Eric. *Twentieth Century Music: An Introduction.* Englewood Cliffs, New Jersey: Prentice-Hall, 1974, 242 pp.

Salzman gives a good account of the development of neoclassicism, serialism, and Gebrauchmusik, and the influence of the schools of thought on American composers.

Thomson, Virgil. *American Music Since 1910.* New York: Holt, Rinehart, and Winston, 1970, 204 pp.

Thomson gives capsule biographies of 106 American composers including Dello Joio (pp. 137–38). Chapters 1 and 2, "America's Musical Maturity" and "America's Musical Traits" are also relevant.

Articles

Affelder, Paul. "The Artists Who Create the Nation's Best Serious Music." *National Observer,* 8 July 1963, p. 18.

The article gives a capsule biography of nine of America's leading composers of serious music. Dello Joio is included.

Clark, Francis. "Questions and Answers." *Clavier* (December 1971): 31–32.

Dello Joio speaks of the role of the performer in the chain of communication between composer and listener.

Downes, Edward. "The Music of Norman Dello Joio." *Musical Quarterly* 48 (April 1962): 149–72.

This article provides an excellent review of Dello Joio's work up to 1961. Important stylistic influences are highlighted in the discussion of his most important works up to that time. A chronological list of works up to 1961 is included, but it is not entirely accurate with respect to some of Dello Joio's early works.

Erickson, Raymond. "He Believes in the Creator." *New York Times,* 9 July 1972, Sect. II, p. 9, col. 1.
Mr. Erickson interviews Dello Joio about the motives behind his move to Boston.

Fuller, Donald. "Bernard Wagenaar, a Portrait." *Modern Music* 21, no. 4 (May–June 1944): 225–31.
This article discusses the musical style of Wagenaar, Dello Joio's composition teacher at Juilliard.

Glanville-Hicks, Peggy. "Dello Joio, Norman." In *Groves Dictionary of Music and Musicians.* Fifth edition, edited by Eric Bloom. New York: St. Martin's Press, 1954.
The article on Dello Joio is a brief biographical sketch. A classified list of works is also included.

Harman, Carter. "Composer of New Opera Discusses His Work." *New York Times,* 7 May 1950, Sect. II, p. 7, col. 1.
The article contains background information on Dello Joio's opera, *The Triumph of Joan.* It also relates some of his views on contemporary opera.

Hinson, Maurice. "The Solo Piano Music of Norman Dello Joio." *American Music Teacher* 19 (1970): 34 + .
This article provides a brief survey of Dello Joio's music for solo piano.

Horst, L. "Composer/Choreographer." *Dance Perspectives* 16 (1963): 18–21.
Dello Joio speaks frankly about the relationship between the composer and choreographer and his own approach to writing music for dance.

Powell, Mel. "Current Chronicle." *Musical Quarterly,* 42 (July 1956): 383–86.
Powell gives an excellent review and brief analysis of *The Trial at Rouen.*

Sabin, Robert. "Norman Dello Joio." In *International Cyclopedia of Music and Musicians.* Ninth edition, edited by Robert Sabin. New York: Dodd, Mead & Co., 1974, 521–23.
This is a brief biographical sketch that mentions important works and stylistic traits of Dello Joio. A list of works up to 1968 is included.

Sabin, Robert. "Norman Dello Joio." *Musical America,* 1 December 1950, pp. 9 + .
Sabin discusses the principle influences on Dello Joio's style.

Schonberg, Harold. "Our Changing Musical Language." *New York Times,* 31 January 1965, Sect. II, p. 11, col. 1.
One of the nation's leading music critics observes a shifting emphasis of musical style toward the more avant-garde practices in the mid-sixties, a tendency that Dello Joio resisted.

Sessions, Roger. "Problems and Issues Facing The Composer Today." In *Problems of Modern Music.* Edited by Paul Henry Lang. New York: W. W. Norton, 1960, 21–33.

Sessions illuminates the difficulties faced by modern composers in coping with such issues as atonality, serialism, and the dehumanization of music, all problems that Dello Joio had to face in the development of his own style.

"Norman Dello Joio." In *Current Biography Yearbook* (1957). Edited by Marjorie Dent Candee. New York: H. W. Wilson, 1957, 138–40.

This is another biographical sketch that mentions Dello Joio's important works up to the mid-fifties.

"Norman Dello Joio." *Inter American Music Bulletin* 9 (1963): 41–50.

This is another biographical sketch that also includes a classified list of works. The dating of several of the works is inaccurate.

"We Salute Norman Dello Joio." *Music Clubs Magazine* 36 (April 1957): 67 + .

This is still another brief biographical sketch that mentions Dello Joio's important works.

Theses and Dissertations

Arlton, Dean Luther. "American Piano Sonatas of the Twentieth Century." Ph.D. dissertation, Columbia University, 1968, 400 pp.
(Microfilm. Ann Arbor: University Microfilms.)
This author provides a penetrating analysis of Dello Joio's third piano sonata.

Bumgardner, Thomas A. "The Solo Vocal Works of Norman Dello Joio." DMA treatise, University of Texas at Austin, 1973, 225 pp.
(Microfilm. Ann Arbor: University Microfilms.)
This treatise provides an in-depth look at the music and poetry of Dello Joio's solo songs.

Del Rosso, Charles F. "A Study of Selected Solo Clarinet Literature of Four American Composers as a Basis for Performance and Teaching." Ph.D. dissertation, Columbia University, 1969, 184 pp.
(Microfilm. Ann Arbor: University Microfilms.)
Del Rosso provides an excellent analysis of the music and performance problems encountered in the *Concertante* for clarinet and piano.

Wannamaker, John S. "The Musical Settings of Walt Whitman." Ph.D. dissertation, University of Minnesota, 1975, 644 pp.
(Microfilm. Ann Arbor: University Microfilms.)
A pioneer effort, this work contains a complete chapter on Dello Joio's Whitman settings for chorus.

Whalen, John R. "A Comparative Study of the *Sonata Number Three* for Piano and the *Variations, Chaconne, and Finale* for Orchestra by Norman Dello Joio." Unpublished doctoral thesis, Indiana University, 1969, 41 pp.
This thesis provides an accurate description of the two works in question, but lacks any in-depth analysis.

Catalog of Musical Works

1937   *Ballad of Thomas Jefferson* for voice and piano. New York: Weaner-Levant, 1943.
Quartet for four bassoons. Unpublished.
Sonata for violin and piano. Unpublished.
Sonata for cello and piano. Unpublished.
Trio for piano, violin, and cello. Unpublished.

1938   *Colloquy* for violin and piano. Unpublished.
Sonata for violin and piano. Unpublished.

1939   *Chicago* for mixed chorus a cappella. Unpublished.
Concertino for flute and strings. Unpublished.
"Gone" for voice and piano. Unpublished.
"Joy" for voice and piano. Unpublished.
"Mill Doors" for voice and piano. New York: Carl Fischer, 1948.
Quartet for flute, oboe, clarinet, and bassoon. Unpublished.

1940   *Ballad* for string orchestra. Unpublished.
Concertino in Stilo Classico for piano and orchestra. Unpublished.
Sinfonietta for orchestra. Unpublished.
Suite for piano. New York: G. Schirmer, 1945.
Trio for clarinet, French horn, and bassoon. Unpublished.

1941   Concerto for two pianos and orchestra. Unpublished.
The Duke of Sacramento, ballet score for two pianos. Unpublished.
Prairie, ballet score for two pianos (the music is the same as *Sinfonietta*). Unpublished.
Spoon River for piano. Unpublished.
Vigil Strange for mixed chorus and piano (four hands). New York: Merrymount Music Corporation, 1943.

1942   *Fantasia on a Gregorian Theme* for violin and piano. New York: Carl Fischer, 1949.
Magnificat for orchestra. New York: G. Schirmer, 1944.

1943   *Greentree Thoroughbred,* film score for orchestra. Unpublished.
The Mystic Trumpeter for mixed chorus and French horn. New York: G. Schirmer, 1945.
Prelude to a Young Dancer for piano. New York: G. Schirmer, 1946.

Prelude to a Young Musician for piano. New York: G. Schirmer, 1945.

Sextet for three recorders and string trio. New York: Hargail Music Press, 1944.

Sonata no. 1 for piano. New York: Hargail Music Press, 1947.

Sonata no. 2 for piano. New York: G. Schirmer, 1948.

To a Lone Sentry for orchestra. New York: G. Schirmer, 1945.

1944   *Concert Music* for orchestra. New York: Carl Fischer, 1949.

Concertino for harmonica and orchestra. Unpublished.

Duo Concertante for two pianos. Unpublished.

Duo Concertato for cello and piano. New York: G. Schirmer, 1949.

Trio for flute, cello, and piano. New York: Carl Fischer, 1948.

1945   Concerto for harp and orchestra. New York: Carl Fischer.

Western Star, symphony for voices and orchestra. Unpublished.

On Stage, ballet score for orchestra. New York: G. Schirmer.

Suite from On Stage for piano. New York: G. Schirmer, 1945.

1946   *A Fable* for mixed chorus and piano. New York: Carl Fischer, 1947.

A Jubilant Song for mixed chorus or women's chorus and piano. New York: G. Schirmer, 1946.

"New Born" for voice and piano. New York: Carl Fischer, 1948.

Nocturne in F-sharp for piano. New York: Carl Fischer, 1950.

"There is a Lady Sweet and Kind" for voice and piano. New York: Carl Fischer, 1948.

Tre Ricercare for piano and orchestra. New York: Carl Fischer.

1947   "The Assassination" for voice and piano. New York. Carl Fischer, 1949.

"Lament" for voice and piano. New York: Carl Fischer, 1949.

Madrigal for mixed chorus and piano. New York: Carl Fischer, 1947.

Sonata no. 3 for piano. New York: Carl Fischer, 1948.

Variations, Chaconne, and Finale for orchestra. New York: Carl Fischer, 1950.

1948   *Diversion of Angels,* ballet score for small orchestra. New York: Carl Fischer.

Serenade (concert version of *Diversion of Angels*) for orchestra. New York: Carl Fischer, 1953.

Six Love Songs for voice and piano. New York: Carl Fischer, 1954.
   1. "Eyebright"
   2. "Why So Pale and Wan, Fond Lover?"
   3. "Meeting at Night"
   4. "The Dying Nightingale"
   5. "All Things Leave Me"
   6. "How Do I Love Thee?"

Variations and Capriccio for violin and piano. New York: Carl Fischer, 1949.

1949   *Concertante* for clarinet and orchestra. New York: Carl Fischer, 1955.

New York Profiles for orchestra. New York: Carl Fischer, 1952.

The Triumph of Joan, opera in three acts. Unpublished.

1950   *The Bluebird* for mixed chorus and piano. New York: Carl Fischer, 1952.

Nocturne in E for piano. New York: Carl Fischer, 1950.

A Psalm of David for mixed chorus, strings, brass, and percussion. New York: Carl Fischer, 1951.

1951   *Epigraph* for orchestra. New York: Carl Fischer, 1953.

The Triumph of Saint Joan Symphony for orchestra. New York: Carl Fischer, 1952.

1952   *Aria and Toccata* for two pianos. New York: Carl Fischer, 1955.

Song of the Open Road for mixed chorus, trumpet, and piano. New York: Carl Fischer, 1953.

1953   *The Ruby,* opera in one act. New York: Deschon Music, Inc., 1955.

Song of Affirmation for mixed chorus, soprano solo, narrator, and orchestra. New York: Carl Fischer, 1953.

Somebody's Coming for mixed chorus and piano. New York: Carl Fischer, 1953.

Sweet Sunny for mixed chorus and piano. New York: Carl Fischer, 1954.

The Tall Kentuckian, incidental music for soloists, chorus, and orchestra. New York: Carl Fischer.

1954   *Adieu, Mignonne, When You Are Gone* for women's chorus and piano. New York: Carl Fischer, 1955.

The Lamentation of Saul for baritone voice, flute, oboe, clarinet, viola, and piano (also scored for full orchestra). New York: Carl Fischer, 1970.

1955   "The Listeners" for voice and piano. New York: Carl Fischer, 1960.

Seraphic Dialogue, ballet performed to the music of *The Triumph of Saint Joan Symphony.*

The Trial at Rouen, opera in two acts. New York: Deshon Music, Inc.

1956   *Meditations on Ecclesiastes* for string orchestra (concert title of the ballet "There is a Time"). New York: Carl Fischer, 1956.

1956–57 *Air Power,* television score for 23 films. Unpublished.

Air Power, symphonic suite for orchestra. New York: Carl Fischer.

1957 *Here Is New York,* television score for CBS-TV. Unpublished.
Ballad of the Seven Lively Arts for piano and orchestra. New York: Carl Fischer.

1958 *O Sing unto the Lord* for male chorus and organ. New York: Carl Fischer, 1959.
To Saint Cecilia for mixed chorus and brass. New York: Carl Fischer, 1958.
The Triumph of Saint Joan, opera in two acts (revised version of *The Trial at Rouen*). New York: Deshon Music, Inc.

1959 "Un Sonetto di Petrarca" for voice and piano. New York: E. B. Marks, 1964.

1960 *America and Americans,* television score for NBC-TV. Unpublished.
"A Christmas Carol" for voice and piano (also for mixed chorus or women's chorus and piano). New York: E. B. Marks, 1967.
Anthony and Cleopatra, incidental music for small orchestra. Unpublished.
Prayers of Cardinal Newman for mixed chorus and organ. New York: Carl Fischer, 1962.
Vanity Fair, television score for CBS-TV. Unpublished.

1961 *Blood Moon,* opera in three acts. Unpublished.
Fantasy and Variations for piano and orchestra. New York: Carl Fischer, 1963.
"The Holy Infant's Lullaby" for voice and piano (also for mixed chorus or women's chorus and piano). New York: E. B. Marks, 1962.
The Saintmaker's Christmas Eve, television score for ABC-TV. Unpublished.

1962 "Bright Star" for voice and piano (also for two voice chorus or mixed chorus SATB and piano). New York: E.B. Marks, 1968.
Family Album for piano (four hands). New York: E. B. Marks, 1962.
Three Songs of Adieu for voice and piano. New York: E. B. Marks, 1962.
Time of Decision, television score for Talent Associates. Unpublished.

1963 *Colloquies* for violin and piano. New York: E. B. Marks, 1964.
Night Song for piano. New York: E. B. Marks, 1965.
Song's End for female chorus and piano. New York: E. B. Marks, 1964.

Variants on a Medieval Tune for band. New York: E. B. Marks, 1963.

1964 *From Every Horizon,* film score for orchestra. Unpublished.

The Louvre, television score for NBC-TV. New York: E. B. Marks.

Suite for the Young for piano. New York: E. B. Marks, 1964.

Three Songs of Chopin for orchestra (also for chorus SA or SATB with orchestral or piano accompaniment). New York: E. B. Marks, 1964.

1965 *Antiphonal Fantasy* for organ, brass, and strings. New York: E. B. Marks, 1966.

From Every Horizon for band. New York: E. B. Marks, 1965.

Laudation for organ. New York: E. B. Marks, 1965.

Scenes from the Louvre for band. New York: E. B. Marks, 1966.

1966 *Five Images* for piano (four hands). New York: E. B. Marks, 1967.

Songs of Walt Whitman for mixed chorus and orchestra (or piano). New York: E. B. Marks, 1966.

1967 *Air for Strings* for string orchestra. New York: E. B. Marks, 1967.

Five Images for orchestra (a transcription of the piano work by the same title). New York: E. B. Marks, 1967.

Proud Music of the Storm for mixed chorus, brass, and organ. New York: E. B. Marks, 1967.

1968 *Capriccio on the Interval of a Second* for piano. New York: E. B. Marks, 1969.

Christmas Music, a transcription of traditional carols for piano-four hands (also for mixed chorus and piano). New York: E. B. Marks, 1968.

Fantasies on a Theme by Haydn for band. New York: E. B. Marks, 1968.

Time of Snow, ballet score for baritone voice and orchestra. Unpublished.

Years of the Modern for mixed chorus, brass, and percussion. New York: E. B. Marks, 1968.

1969 *Bagatelles* for harp. New York: E. B. Marks, 1969.

Homage to Haydn for orchestra. New York: E. B. Marks.

Mass for mixed chorus, brass, and organ. New York: E. B. Marks, 1969.

"Note Left on a Doorstep" for voice and piano. New York: E. B. Marks, 1969.

Songs of Abelard for baritone solo and band (a transcription of the ballet *Time of Snow*). New York: E. B. Marks, 1969.

1970   *Evocations* for mixed chorus and orchestra (or piano). New York: E. B. Marks, 1970.
      I. "Visitants at Night"
      II. "Promise of Spring"

1971   *All Is Still,* monodrama for tenor solo and chamber ensemble. Unpublished.
    Lyric Pieces for the Young for piano. New York: E. B. Marks, 1971.

1972   *Choreography* for string orchestra. New York: E. B. Marks, 1972.
    Come to Me My Love for mixed chorus and piano. New York: E. B. Marks, 1973.
    Concertante for Wind Instruments for band. New York: E. B. Marks, 1973.
    The Developing Flutist, suite for flute and piano. New York: E. B. Marks, 1972.
    Of Crows and Clusters for mixed chorus and piano. New York: E. B. Marks, 1972.
    Psalm of Peace for mixed chorus, trumpet, French horn, and organ. New York: E. B. Marks, 1972.

1973   *Leisure* for mixed chorus and piano. New York: Associated Music Publishers, 1975.
    Lyric Fantasies for viola and string orchestra (or string quintet). New York: Associated Music Publishers, 1975.
    The Poet's Song for mixed chorus and piano. New York: Associated Music Publishers, 1974.

1974   *Stage Parodies* for piano (four hands). New York: Associated Music Publishers, 1975.
    Three Essays for clarinet and piano. New York: E. B. Marks, 1974.
    Thezmophoriazousae, incidental music for soloists, chorus, and orchestra. Unpublished.

1975   *Diversions* for piano. New York: E. B. Marks, 1975.
    Five Lyric Pieces for the Young Organist for organ (a transcription of *Diversions*). New York: E. B. Marks, 1975.
    Mass in Honor of the Blessed Virgin Mary for cantor, congregation, and three part mixed choir with organ (optional brass) accompaniment. New York: Associated Music Publishers, 1975.
    Mass in Honor of the Eucharist for cantor, congregation, four part mixed choir, and organ. New York: Associated Music Publishers, 1976.
    Notes from Tom Paine for mixed chorus a cappella. New York: Associated Music Publishers, 1975.

Satiric Dances for a Comedy by Aristophanes for band. New York: Associated Music Publishers, 1975.

1976   *Colonial Ballads* for band. New York: Associated Music Publishers, 1979.

Colonial Variants for orchestra. New York: Associated Music Publishers, 1978.

Songs of Remembrance for baritone voice and orchestra. New York: Associated Music Publishers, 1979.

Southern Echoes for orchestra. New York: Associated Music Publishers.

1978   *Arietta* for string orchestra. New York: E. B. Marks, 1978.

Caccia for band (a transcription of no. 3 of *Diversions*). New York: E. B. Marks, 1978.

Concertante for chamber orchestra (a transcription of *Lyric Fantasies*). New York: Associated Music Publishers.

1979   *As of a Dream,* a masque on poetry of Walt Whitman for narrator, mixed chorus, soloists, optional dancers, and orchestra. New York: Associated Music Publishers, 1983.

The Dancing Sergeant for band (a transcription from *Five Images*). New York: E. B. Marks, 1979.

Hymns without Words for mixed chorus and orchestra. New York: Associated Music Publishers, 1981.

The Psalmist's Meditation for mixed chorus and piano. New York: Associated Music Publishers, 1981.

Salute to Scarlatti for harpischord or piano. New York: Associated Music Publishers, 1980.

Sonata for trumpet and piano. New York: Associated Music Publishers, 1980.

1980   *Concert Variants* for piano. New York: Associated Music Publishers, 1983.

1981   *Ballabili* for orchestra. New York: Associated Music Publishers, 1983.

1982   *Love Songs at Parting* for mixed chorus and piano. New York: Associated Music Publishers, 1984.

Reflections on an Original Christmas Tune for wind quintet. New York: Associated Music Publishers.

Discography

Aria and Toccata for two pianos. T. & R. Grunschlag. CRISD–472

Air for Strings. Lowell E. Graham conducting the United States Air Force String Orchestra. Golden Crest USAF–101878–B (1978).

Air Power-Symphonic Suite. Eugene Ormandy conducting the Philadelphia Orchestra. Columbia MS 6029 (1957).

Blood Moon. San Francisco Opera Company conducted by Leopold Ludwig. Four Track 71/2 ips. stereo. Orchard Collection, Indiana University (1961).

Choreography. Norman Dello Joio conducting the National ASTA Orchestra. Golden Crest.

Colonial Ballads. Gary Garner conducting the West Texas State University Symphonic Band. Golden Crest ATH 5054 (1978).

Come to Me My Love. Norman Dello Joio conducting the Boston University Choruses. Golden Crest ATH 5059 (1978).

Concertante for Clarinet and Piano. John Russo, clarinet; Lydia Walton Ignacio, piano. Orion ORS 79330 (1979).

Concertante for Wind Instruments. Gary Garner conducting the West Texas State University Symphonic Band. Golden Crest ATH 5054 (1978).

Concerto for Harp and Orchestra. Thomas Scherman conducting the Little Orchestra Society. Edward Vito, harp. Columbia ML 4303.

The Developing Flutist. Laila Pador, flute; Anita Swearengin, piano. Laurel Protone LP–14 (1976).

Duo Concertante for Cello and Piano. Jeffrey Solow, cello; Albert Dominguez, piano. Pelican LP 2010 (1979).

Epigraph. Hans Swarowsky conducting the Vienna Symphony Orchestra. Desto DST 6416 (1965).

Fantasy and Variations for Piano and Orchestra. Erich Leinsdorf conducting the Boston Symphony Orchestra. Lorin Hollander, piano. RCA Victor LSC 2667 (1963).

Fantasies on a Theme by Haydn. Gary Garner conducting the West Texas State University Symphonic Band. Golden Crest ATH 5054 (1978).

From Every Horizon. Gary Garner conducting the West Texas State University Symphonic Band. Golden Crest ATH 5054 (1978).

Homage to Haydn. Leonard Slatkin conducting the Louisville Orchestra. Louisville LS 742 (1974).

A Jubilant Song. Jerold D. Ottley conducting the Mormon Tabernacle Choir. Columbia M34134 (1976).

Mass in Honor of the Eucharist. Norman Dello Joio conducting the Boston University Choruses. Golden Crest ATH 5059 (1978).

The Listeners. William Parker, baritone; Dalton Baldwin, piano. New World Records NW 300 (1978).

Meditations on Ecclesiastes. 1. Alfredo Antonini conducting the Oslo Philharmonic Orchestra. Composers Recordings, Inc. CRI SRD 110. 2. Nicholas Harsanyi conducting the Princeton Chamber Orchestra. Decca DL 10138 (1967). 3. Joseph Silverstein conducting the Boston University Symphony Orchestra. Boston University BU 101 (1976).

New York Profiles. Arthur Bennet Lipkin conducting the Oslo Philharmonic Orchestra. Composers Recordings, Inc. CRI SD 209.

Nocturnes (2) For Piano. Grant Johannesen, piano. Golden Crest CRS 4111.

Notes From Tom Paine. On "A Bicentennial Celebration." Columbia M33838 (1976).

Of Crows and Clusters. Norman Dello Joio conducting the Boston University Choruses. Golden Crest ATH 5059 (1978).

The Poet's Song. Norman Dello Joio conducting the Boston University Choruses. Golden Crest ATH 5059 (1978).

A Psalm of David. Helen Hosmer conducting the Crane Chorus and Orchestra. Concert Hall Society CHS 1113.

The Ruby. Indiana University Opera Theatre. Four track 71/2 ips. stereo. Orchard Collection, Indiana University (1955).

Satiric Dances. Gary Garner conducting the West Texas State University Symphonic Band. Golden Crest ATH 5054 (1978).

Scenes from The Louvre. Norman Dello Joio conducting the Baldwin-Wallace College Concert Band. Century Records 25856 (1969).

Serenade. Hans Swarowsky conducting the Vienna Symphony Orchestra. Desto DST 6413 (1965).

Sonata No. 3 for Piano. Frank Glazer, piano. Concert Disc CS–1217 (1960). Del Purves, piano. Music Library Recording 2439.

Sonata for Trumpet and Piano. David Hickman, trumpet; Eric Dalheim, piano. Crystal Records (1981).

Song of Affirmation. Norman Dello Joio conducting the West Hartford, Connecticut Public School Choirs. Vogt Quality Records.

Song of the Open Road. Norman Dello Joio conducting the Boston University Choruses. Golden Crest ATH 5059 (1978).

Songs of the Abelard. Norman Dello Joio conducting the Baldwin-Wallace College Concert Band. Century Records 25856.

To Saint Cecilia. T. Wright conducting the Columbia University Chapel Choir. Kapp LP9057.

The Trial at Rouen. NBC-TV Opera Theatre. Four track 71/2 ips. stereo. Orchard Collection, Indiana University (1956).

Triumph of Saint Joan Symphony. Robert Whitney conducting the Louisville Orchestra. Columbia Special Products AML4615 (1974).

Trio for Flute, Cello, and Piano. LeRoy, Foster, Scholz Trio. Concert Hall Society CHS (1947).

Variants on a Medieval Tune. Paul Bryan conducting the Duke University Concert Band. Century Records 39239 (1970).

Variations and Capriccio. Patricia Travers, violin; Norman Dello Joio, piano. Columbia Special Products AML 4845 (1974).

Variations, Chaconne, and Finale. Eugene Ormandy conducting the Philadelphia Orchestra. Columbia ML 5263 (1958).

Index